The Letter to the Galatians

OneBook.

DAILY–WEEKLY

The Letter to the Galatians

David A. deSilva

Printed in the United States of America

Cover design by Strange Last Name
Page design by PerfecType, Nashville, Tennessee

DeSilva, David Arthur.
The Letter to the Galatians / David A. deSilva. – Franklin, Tennessee : Seedbed Publishing, ©2019.

pages ; cm. + 1 videodisc – (OneBook. Daily-weekly)

ISBN 9781628246919 (paperback)
ISBN 9781628246957 (DVD)
ISBN 9781628246926 (Mobi)
ISBN 9781628246933 (ePub)
ISBN 9781628246940 (uPDF)

1. Bible. Galatians -- Textbooks. 2. Bible. Galatians -- Study and teaching.
3. Bible. Galatians -- Commentaries. I. Title. II. Series.

BS2685.6.D47 2019 227/.406 2019953016

SEEDBED PUBLISHING
Franklin, Tennessee
seedbed.com

CONTENTS

WELCOME TO ONEBOOK DAILY-WEEKLY

John Wesley, in a letter to one of his leaders, penned the following:

> O begin! Fix some part of every day for private exercises. You may acquire the taste which you have not: what is tedious at first, will afterwards be pleasant. Whether you like it or not, read and pray daily. It is for your life; there is no other way; else you will be a trifler all your days. . . . Do justice to your own soul; give it time and means to grow. Do not starve yourself any longer. Take up your cross and be a Christian altogether.

Rarely are our lives most shaped by our biggest ambitions and highest aspirations. Rather, our lives are most shaped, for better or for worse, by those small things we do every single day.

At Seedbed, our biggest ambition and highest aspiration is to resource the followers of Jesus to become lovers and doers of the Word of God every single day, to become people of One Book.

To that end, we have created the OneBook Daily-Weekly. First, it's important to understand what this is not: warm, fuzzy, sentimental devotions. If you engage the Daily-Weekly for any length of time, you will learn the Word of God. You will grow profoundly in your love for God, and you will become a passionate lover of people.

How Does the Daily-Weekly Work?

Daily. As the name implies, every day invites a short but substantive engagement with the Bible. Five days a week you will read a passage of Scripture followed by a short segment of teaching and closing with questions for refection and self-examination. On the sixth day, you will review and reflect on the previous five days.

Weekly. Each week, on the seventh day, find a way to gather with at least one other person doing the study. Pursue the weekly guidance for gathering. Share learning, insight, encouragement, and most important, how the Holy Spirit is working in your lives.

That's it. Depending on the length of the study, when the eight or twelve weeks are done, we will be ready with the next study. On an ongoing basis, we will release new editions of the Daily-Weekly. Over time, those who pursue this course of learning will develop a rich library of Bible learning resources for the long haul.

OneBook Daily-Weekly will develop eight- and twelve-week studies that cover the entire Old and New Testaments. Seedbed will publish new studies regularly so that an ongoing supply of group lessons will be available. All titles will remain accessible, which means they can be used in any order that fits your needs or the needs of your group.

If you are looking for a substantive study to learn Scripture through a steadfast method, look no further.

WEEK ONE

Galatians 1:1–10

The One and Only Gospel

ONE

Who Speaks for *God*?

Galatians 1:1 *Paul an apostle—sent neither by human commission nor from human authorities, but through Jesus Christ and God the Father, who raised him from the dead—*

Key Observation. Only the apostolic gospel that faithfully preserves God's invitation, issued on God's terms, has the power to lead us to life.

Understanding the Word. Galatians is one of Paul's most passionately written letters. Some of his converts in the cities of Galatia are being won over by other Jewish Christian teachers who have come along after Paul's departure. These teachers have very different ideas about where to draw the boundaries around the people of God. They also differ significantly concerning the role the law of Moses ought to play in Christian life. They are taking advantage of Paul's absence to pull the Galatian Christians in a very different direction from the course on which Paul had set them. Paul's own authority has come under fire in the process. The new teachers may not have anything against Paul personally. However, they will no doubt have found it necessary to call Paul's motives, credibility, and correctness into question if they are going to win over his converts. The stakes are very high for Paul. From what he hears about the situation, he believes that following the rival teachers' recommendations for moving forward will essentially mean renouncing Jesus and his death on their behalf. He will dramatically warn his converts: "You are cut off from Christ! . . . You fell from grace!" (Gal. 5:4, author's translation).

Paul comes out fighting from the very first sentence. A typical letter in the first-century Roman world would have begun: "Paul to the churches in Galatia, greetings." Every expansion of and departure from the standard form would have been heard as significant. Paul's first expansion asserts that the origin of his commission and the agent through whom his commission came are divine. He does not come to Galatia as the representative of any human group, including the circle of the original apostles in Jerusalem. He comes to represent God and to communicate God's astounding offer of gracious favor. This offer includes reconciliation with God through God's Son, reception of God's transforming Spirit, and rescue thereby from "the present evil age" (1:4). The rival teachers may have come claiming to represent the Jerusalem apostles. If Paul's message does not align with theirs, however, this doesn't mean that Paul has departed from *his* commission and *his* Commissioner. Paul will support this bold claim at some length in 1:10–2:14.

Paul no doubt has strong feelings about rival teachers leading his converts down a different path. He is not immune to turf issues (see 2 Corinthians 10:13–16). He sees enough of the big picture, however, not to be *merely* concerned with defending turf (see Philippians 1:15–18). Paul believes that the rival teachers in Galatia have missed the essential point. They fail to perceive the significance of Jesus' death and resurrection for defining the people of God and for discovering the path to justification before God. Paul will fight to keep his converts grounded in the gospel that *God* has given him for them. He does not want them to set aside *God's* grace and power (2:21). The rival teachers' gospel will give them neither a reliable vision for, nor the spiritual power to attain, the transformation God sought to work in God's "new creation" (Gal. 6:15).

1. What are some areas in which you, your congregation, or your denomination struggle to discern *God's* good news from human distortions of the good news?
2. What do you do to help make sure that you're following a divinely authorized message as gospel and as a reliable pointer to holiness, and not merely a human invention?

TWO
All in the Family

Galatians 1:2 *and all the members of God's family who are with me, To the churches of Galatia:*

Key Observation. When we join ourselves to Christ, we become part of a global family. We inherit all the mutual obligations and support that natural sisters and brothers ought to share.

Understanding the Word. Paul often names teammates who are working alongside him as cosenders of his letters. We encounter Sosthenes as a cosender of 1 Corinthians, Timothy as a cosender of 2 Corinthians, and both Silvanus and Timothy as cosenders of 1 Thessalonians. Galatians is distinctive among his letters. He doesn't name a coauthor, but he also doesn't write as if acting on his own either (as in Romans and Ephesians). Instead, he enlists the support of "all the members of God's family who are with me." He reminds the Galatians that his gospel is not his own invention. It is the gospel embraced by a significant number of those whom God has called together in Christ.

The New Revised Standard Version (NRSV) reads "all the members of God's family who are with me." We could read this more closely as "all the brothers and sisters who are with me." Paul consistently speaks about Christians as a group of siblings. He constantly reinforces the conviction that those whom God has gathered together in Christ form a new family. This family is as real as any family related by blood. Indeed, it *is* related by blood; namely, the blood of Jesus. One Father unites all members together by their adoption into a global "household of faith" (1:3; 4:4–7; 6:10 ESV). Paul leads them, as a new family, to adopt a new ethos and to accept new obligations to one another. They are called to set aside competition, manipulation, deceit, and all the behaviors accepted as appropriate among people who are strangers and outsiders. Instead, they are to give one another the gifts of cooperation, trust, truth-telling, loyalty, and sharing resources (see Colossians 3:5–17; Hebrews 13:1–3, 15–16). They are to invest themselves in advancing one another's interests, not in advancing their individual interests at another's expense (see Philippians 2:3–4). Learning to see and care for one another as family is the backbone of early Christian identity and community.

The fact that Christians meet together in the homes of the wealthier members of the group may make it easier to think of one's fellow Christians as the "household of faith." The Greek *ekklēsiai,* traditionally rendered "churches" (as in Galatians 1:2), is better rendered "assemblies" or "gatherings." There are no churches in the sense of designated buildings in the first century. There are only gatherings of believers in homes (see Romans 16:4–5, 23; 1 Corinthians 16:19; Colossians 4:15; Philemon 2). It is to such gatherings that Paul sends his letter.

Most commentaries on Galatians include a lengthy discussion of *where* in the vast Roman province of Galatia Paul's addressees are located. This also involves discussions of where in the time line of Paul's ministry this letter and the situation it addresses should be placed. I believe that a solid case can be made for identifying these congregations with those Paul and Barnabas planted together on their first joint mission recounted in Acts 13–14. I imagine Galatians being written to the churches in Pisidian Antioch, Iconium, Lystra, and Derbe. Galatians may also be Paul's earliest surviving letter.

1. How can an awareness of what Christians have believed across the ages and across the continents help you avoid local and modern innovations that might distort the gospel?
2. When have you been a part of Christian groups that shared the level of intimacy and mutual commitment that we would associate with a well-functioning family? What facilitated or impeded this?

THREE

Redemption, Rescue, and Response

Galatians 1:3–5 *Grace to you and peace from God our Father and the Lord Jesus Christ, [4]who gave himself for our sins to set us free from the present evil age, according to the will of our God and Father, [5]to whom be the glory forever and ever. Amen.*

Key Observation. Christian life is a life of responding gratefully to Jesus' self-giving love. It is the grateful acceptance of freedom from being dominated by all the powers of this age, including sin, death, the flesh, and Satan.

Understanding the Word. The typical letter opened with the formula: "Sender to Recipient, Greetings." Paul consistently replaces the formal "greetings" with a wish for "grace and peace" to rest upon his addressees. *Grace* is the watchword for this letter. It is centrally at stake in the Galatians' situation (2:21; 5:2–4); it is what Paul desperately wants his converts to continue to experience (1:3; 6:18).

Peace is a watchword of Roman imperial propaganda. Augustus and his successors justify their power based on the peace that they have brought to the Mediterranean, whether through conquest, suppression of revolt, or elimination of pirates and brigands. Paul suggests that peace must come from a different source. It must come from God the Father and the Lord Jesus, who will usher in a new order under new leadership. In God's kingdom, peace will be genuine and not a mere campaign slogan (see 1 Thessalonians 1:9–10).

Paul opens by reminding his hearers of the display of grace at the core of the Christian confession. Jesus gave himself for the sins we committed (see also Galatians 2:19–21; 3:10–14; 4:4–5). Both Jews and Greeks are familiar with stories of righteous, innocent people who gave up their lives for the sake of others. Jews especially remember the faithful who allowed themselves to be tortured to death rather than break faith with God's covenant. They have already interpreted the deaths of these martyrs as an offering of obedience to God on behalf of the whole people. These martyrs atoned for the disobedient and turning God's wrath to mercy (see 4 Maccabees 6:28–30; 17:21–22). Jesus is such a benefactor and more, as Paul will remind his converts throughout this letter. Such selfless generosity on Jesus' part demands absolute loyalty and gratitude in response, as Paul will also remind his converts (see 2 Corinthians 5:14–15).

Jesus' death is not just a *ransom* for sins, but a *rescue* from "the present evil age" (1:4). Roman propaganda speaks of life under Augustus and his successors as the return of a Golden Age. Paul has a very different outlook. While God had created everything "good" (Gen. 1:4, 10, 12, etc.), the whole cosmos is perverted by human and angelic disobedience. Human beings labor under the oppressive powers of sin, death, flesh, and the devil. But Jesus' death and resurrection signal the end of this present evil age. It signals the dawning of the age to come, in which God's good vision for human existence will come to full fruition. It is a decisive turning point in God's dealings with human beings, ushering in a new era of freedom that the Holy Spirit is already making real in the lives of Christ's own and in the new community forming in his name.

All of this is the outworking of "the will of our God and Father" (1:4). If we see in Jesus' death a man's attempt to appease an angry God on our behalf, we need to look again. Paul will have us see, in Jesus' death, a generous God's invitation to his alienated creatures both to return to his favor and to move forward together into the new creation where all will be restored.

1. How fully does Jesus' *giving* of his life for you shape your *living* of your life for him? In what specific ways?
2. Where do you fall on the spectrum of seeking rescue "from the present evil age" and seeking rootedness and fulfillment in this age? How does this correlate to your investment of yourself in your own transformation, in Christian community, and in mission?

FOUR

The Other Gospel

Galatians 1:6–7 *I am astonished that you are so quickly deserting the one who called you in the grace of Christ and are turning to a different gospel—[7]not that there is another gospel, but there are some who are confusing you and want to pervert the gospel of Christ.*

Key Observation. The apostolic gospel that positions us to live in line with God's Holy Spirit is the only *genuine* good news.

Understanding the Word. The core of the problem in Galatia is the proclamation there of a very "different gospel" (1:6). Paul and the rival teachers who follow him to Galatia can agree that Jesus' death and resurrection was an act of decisive importance in God's dealings with humanity. They can agree that it sounded the call to gather all the nations to worship the one God. They disagree, however, as to the response that God seeks to this call.

The rival teachers believe that circumcision is the way all people, Jew or Gentile, join themselves to God's people and number themselves among Abraham's heirs (see Genesis 17:9–14). Jesus' death indeed cleanses both Jew and Gentile from their past sins, but for the purpose of a fresh opportunity to take on the yoke of God's eternal covenant. The law of Moses remains the means to "choose life" (Deut. 30:15–20). This Law is God's provision for mastering the passions and desires of the flesh. It is the path to experiencing freedom at last from the power of sin and to attaining a consistent life of righteousness (see 4 Maccabees 1:13–17; 5:22–24). Like Paul, these rival teachers believe in the unity of the one body of the church. Unlike Paul, they believe that the Gentiles need to adapt their practice to the Jewish way of life in order to enjoy that unity of fellowship.

Paul's rivals promote obedience to the Torah as the perfect way to complement and complete the Galatians' faith in Jesus. Paul, however, presents this course of action as the desertion and rejection of their divine patron (1:6). He opens the body of his letter by expressing his shock that his converts are contemplating such an ugly course of action to so generous a Savior. He uses words that have become standard by his time for expressing a rebuke. He adds to their shame by highlighting the ease with which they were allowing themselves to be turned aside. How could they be "so quickly" diverted from the noble course on which Paul, acting on God's behalf, has set them?

Paul quickly shifts from calling the rival teachers' message "a different gospel" to denying that it even qualifies as "another gospel." Paul brings a message to the Galatians that God has validated by pouring out his Holy Spirit upon them. A "*different* gospel" (1:6, author's emphasis) therefore turns out to be "no gospel at all" (1:7). The rival teachers have gotten the gospel *sufficiently* wrong to have gotten it *all* wrong, as Paul will explain at length (2:15–5:12).

We need to be careful not to imitate the rival teachers in their mishandling of the good news. They have a stack of scriptures on their side. Indeed, they have many more than Paul has, if the truth be told. They have a wealth of tradition and history on their side. What they lack, however, is all important—an appreciation of the value and the reliability of the Holy Spirit, that "best gift divine"[1] secured for us by Jesus (3:13–14), as the guide and guardian of God's work on this side of Christ's coming.

1. To what extent do you rely on traditional or scriptural rules to make decisions? To what extent do you rely on the Holy Spirit's leading?
2. Where do you find temptations to pervert the gospel of Christ in your setting? (Try to think here not only of perversions of the gospel that you oppose, but of perversions of the gospel that you embrace!)

FIVE

The Integrity of Message and Messenger

Galatians 1:8–10 *But even if we or an angel from heaven should proclaim to you a gospel contrary to what we proclaimed to you, let that one be accursed! [9]As we have said before, so now I repeat, if anyone proclaims to you a gospel contrary to what you received, let that one be accursed!*

[10]Am I now seeking human approval, or God's approval? Or am I trying to please people? If I were still pleasing people, I would not be a servant of Christ.

Key Observation. We must take great care not to deform or reduce the gospel either for the sake of our cherished traditions or our desire to please people.

Understanding the Word. Paul's rebuke builds up to a solemn curse upon anyone who comes along trying to turn Christ's good news into something that it is not. The word rendered *accursed* here is used in other contexts to speak of someone or something that has been consigned to destruction. In Deuteronomy, Moses warns the people of Israel not to shelter anything that God has destined for destruction. If they do so, they will bring destruction on themselves as well (see Deuteronomy 7:26). At Jericho, Achan keeps some of the Canaanites' possessions instead of destroying them as God commanded. As a result, he brings death upon himself and his family (see Joshua 6:18; 7:1–26).

1. Folliott S. Pierpoint, "For the Beauty of the Earth," 1864.

The goal of these commands is to save Israel from bad influences and false teaching (see Deuteronomy 20:16–18).

The significance of Paul's curses is clear. Preserving the contours of God's message of deliverance is of utmost importance. Perverting those contours is the gravest offense. Why? Misrepresenting God will lead untold numbers astray. It will cause them to miss the deliverance that God holds out to them—a deliverance that has cost no less than God the Son's giving himself over to death on their behalf. It is noteworthy that Paul places himself under the same threat. The message authorizes the messenger, not the other way around. Paul must hold himself also to remaining true and steadfast in his proclamation of *God's* message.

Paul's curse calls us to be watchful in regard to the gospel we embrace *and* the gospel we promote! The rival teachers' mistake is to limit the Spirit's flow to the well-worn channels of the Torah. This should make us careful not to insist that the practices that *we* embrace as ways to honor God are the *only* ways real Christians can honor God. We also need to exercise care not to build false boundaries within which the Spirit must flow (as if we could control that!). At the same time, we need to observe the boundaries within which the Spirit *does* work his full transformation of our lives and relationships.

Paul's spirited objections in 1:10 seem to come out of nowhere. Paul is probably responding to something the rival teachers have been saying about him. We don't have to imagine malice on their part. It is enough that they have had to explain to Paul's converts why Paul didn't tell them about the importance of getting circumcised and taking on the Torah's yoke: "Paul's an energetic evangelist, but he's too keen on winning people over to tell them the *whole* truth about what God requires."

Paul affirms that he is not out to talk God and humanity into some workable compromise. He has faithfully declared the message that God gave him and he trusts God's Holy Spirit to carry conviction home. (His bold opening in Galatians should be proof enough of this!) He knows that he can't serve Christ wholeheartedly and consistently and be a slave to public opinion at the same time. We, too, need to discover how to remove all unnecessary stumbling blocks between God's transforming work and the people around us. We also need to allow all *necessary* stumbling blocks to remain in place, to poke, and to provoke the necessary change in all of us if we are to become God's "new creation" (6:15).

1. Where are the absolute boundaries of Christian faith and practice to be drawn? Where is there wiggle room or room for toleration of diversity?
2. When has your desire for acceptance or affirmation from people stopped you from witnessing to God's whole truth?

WEEK ONE

GATHERING DISCUSSION OUTLINE

A. **Open session in prayer.** Ask that God would astonish us anew with fresh insight from God's Word and transform us into the disciples that Jesus desires us to become.

B. **View the video for this week's readings.**

C. What were key insights or takeaways that you gained from your reading during the week and from watching the video commentary? In particular, how did these help you to grow in your faith and understanding of Scripture this week? What parts of the Bible lesson or study raised questions for you?

D. **Discuss selected questions from the daily readings.** Invite class members to share key insights or to raise questions that they found to be the most meaningful.

1. **KEY OBSERVATION:** Only the apostolic gospel that faithfully preserves God's invitation, issued on God's terms, has the power to lead us to life.

   DISCUSSION QUESTION: What do you do to help make sure that you're following a divinely authorized message as gospel and as a reliable pointer to holiness, and not merely a human invention?

2. **KEY OBSERVATION:** When we join ourselves to Christ, we become part of a global family. We inherit all the mutual obligations and support that natural sisters and brothers ought to share.

DISCUSSION QUESTION: When have you been a part of Christian groups that shared the level of intimacy and mutual commitment that we would associate with a well-functioning family? What facilitated or impeded this?

3. **KEY OBSERVATION:** Christian life is a life of responding gratefully to Jesus' self-giving love. It is the grateful acceptance of freedom from being dominated by all the powers of this age, including sin, death, the flesh, and Satan.

   DISCUSSION QUESTION: How fully does Jesus' *giving* of his life for you shape your *living* of your life for him? In what specific ways?

4. **KEY OBSERVATION:** The apostolic gospel that positions us to live in line with God's Holy Spirit is the only *genuine* good news.

   DISCUSSION QUESTION: To what extent do you rely on traditional or scriptural rules to make decisions? To what extent do you rely on the Holy Spirit's leading?

5. **KEY OBSERVATION:** We must take great care not to deform or reduce the gospel either for the sake of our cherished traditions or our desire to please people.

   DISCUSSION QUESTION: When has your desire for acceptance or affirmation from people stopped you from witnessing to God's whole truth?

E. **As the study concludes, consider specific ways that this week's Bible lessons invite you to grow and call you to change.** How do they call us to think differently? How do they challenge us to change in order to align ourselves with God's work in the world? What specific actions should we take to apply the insights of the lesson into our daily lives? What kind of person does our Bible lesson call us to become?

F. **Close session with prayer.** Emphasize God's ongoing work of transformation in our lives in preparation for loving mission and service in the world. Pray for missing class members as well as for persons whom we need to invite to join our study.

WEEK TWO

Galatians 1:11–2:10

A Reliable Messenger with a Reliable Message

ONE

Consider the Source

Galatians 1:11–12 ESV *For I would have you know, brothers, that the gospel that was preached by me is not man's gospel. [12]For I did not receive it from any man, nor was I taught it, but I received it through a revelation of Jesus Christ.*

Key Observation. Paul's gospel message has its roots in God's revealing to him who Jesus Christ really was—something no human being had been able to do.

Understanding the Word. Paul reveals a great deal about his own story in the opening chapters of Galatians. These episodes are interesting as windows into the life of a towering figure of the early church. However, we shouldn't lose sight of the reasons Paul brings up these episodes and shapes them as he does. Each episode contributes to a case that Paul is making to answer an essential question: Why should the Galatians trust Paul over the rival teachers? Paul's narrative establishes four important points. First, the message that Paul preaches comes from an encounter with the glorified Christ, not from human teachers. His proclamation of God's good news must be given more weight than the rival teachers' message. Second, Paul's authority and commission come from God and not from the Jerusalem apostles. He is not dependent upon them nor does he answer to them. Third, Paul has nevertheless acted collegially toward the Jerusalem apostles, and they have recognized his work and message as valid. Finally, Paul is the one apostle who has consistently stood up for "the truth of the gospel" (2:5, 14) and not caved in to pressure from other people. The Galatians should believe, therefore, that Paul will do the same in the present conflict.

Paul returns in 1:11–12 to the claim he made at the letter's outset. In the opening verse he called himself "an apostle—not from men nor through man, but through Jesus Christ and God the Father" (1:1 ESV). Here he claims the same regarding the gospel message that he brought to Galatia. This is admittedly a bold claim. We would surely and rightly question anyone who came into our churches making such a claim! In our present situation, it is usually the *false* apostle who claims God as the direct source of his or her new message. Paul, however, will immediately offer some convincing evidence to support his claim. The proof is in his own story of transformation. Only God's intervention could explain how the most fanatical persecutor of the Christ cult became its most passionate promoter.

Today's verses begin to explain how Paul pronounced a curse upon anyone who promoted a different message. Any gospel that differs from the message Paul brought to the Galatians sets itself against the message Paul received from God. Paul didn't learn this message from some group of human beings. It wasn't the result of careful negotiations with other apostles and stakeholders. It certainly was not a message that Paul invented, for he had been investing his own life in a completely different direction. It was a message that God *imposed* upon Paul.

The key phrase is "through a revelation of Jesus Christ." The New International Version (NIV) understands the Greek to mean that Jesus Christ is the source of the revelation: "by revelation *from* Jesus Christ" (author's emphasis). It seems more likely that Paul came upon his understanding of the gospel because God unveiled for him who Jesus Christ really was. This new understanding is reflected in every chapter of Galatians. Paul's faithfulness to this revelation and to the God who revealed his Son to Paul (1:16) is the most important answer to the question: Why should the Galatians trust Paul?

1. How have other people, and how has God, contributed to opening your eyes to who Jesus Christ really is?
2. What merely human gospels have you encountered? What helps you recognize when a so-called gospel is merely a human-made message?

TWO
Paul's About-Face

Galatians 1:13–17 ESV *For you have heard of my former life in Judaism, how I persecuted the church of God violently and tried to destroy it. [14]And I was advancing in Judaism beyond many of my own age among my people, so extremely zealous was I for the traditions of my fathers. [15]But when he who had set me apart before I was born, and who called me by his grace, [16]was pleased to reveal his Son to me, in order that I might preach him among the Gentiles, I did not immediately consult with anyone; [17]nor did I go up to Jerusalem to those who were apostles before me, but I went away into Arabia, and returned again to Damascus.*

Key Observation. When Paul was most on fire for the Law, he found himself most out of alignment with God's righteousness.

Understanding the Word. An object in motion will remain in motion in the same direction unless acted on by an unbalanced force. This is one of the basic principles we learn in high school science class. For one stretch of time, Paul was in motion on a clear trajectory that he describes as "advancing in Judaism" and "persecu[ting] the church of God." In a subsequent stretch of time, Paul was moving on a very different, indeed an opposite, trajectory. The existence of the effect proclaims the existence of the cause. God, the ultimate unbalanced force, had acted upon Paul.

In his former life, Paul had been on fire for God's covenant with Israel. He believed the blessings and curses of Deuteronomy. If Israel kept faith with God by living in line with the Law, God would protect, prosper, and restore Israel. If Israel broke faith with God by neglecting the Law, Israel would continue to experience God's curses (including being ruled by a Gentile superpower). Keeping the covenant was a matter of national security. Paul showed his zeal for the Law in two ways. First, he pressed further than his peers to discover how to bring more and more of his daily practices in line with the Jewish law, the Torah. Second, he applied significant pressure on deviant Jews to observe the Torah more strictly and carefully (see Philippians 3:6). He had good role models to follow. Phinehas had shown zeal for the Lord by executing an

Israelite together with his Midianite concubine (see Numbers 25:1–13). Elijah had shown zeal by slaughtering the priests of Baal who had been misleading Israel (see 1 Kings 18:40; 19:10). The role of watchdog for the covenant had a fine pedigree.

Enter the unbalanced force. Paul does not give any particulars of how God revealed his Son to him. Indeed, Paul's principal point is what he did *not* do in response to this life-changing event. He did *not* seek clarity about the encounter or his commission from the Jerusalem apostles. He had received a clear impression of the good news and its significance in his encounter with the glorified Jesus. He allowed that impression to gel as he spent three years in Arabia and Damascus. During this time, Paul had begun to fulfill God's commission. He was preaching the gospel in Damascus (see Acts 9:19b–25; 2 Corinthians 11:30–33) and may have done so in Arabia as well, in the cities of the Nabatean kingdom.

Paul's unique experience led him to his most distinctive insights concerning the role of the Torah in God's plan. Specifically, it led him to discover that, in Jesus, God was doing a new thing *apart from* the Torah. When he was most devoted to the Torah, he found himself most directly opposed to God. As he was lining up more and more closely with the Torah, he found himself most *out* of alignment with what God was doing. Having defined righteousness in terms of observing and enforcing the Torah, Paul had joined in condemning God's Righteous One. To encounter Jesus as resurrected could only mean, for Paul, that God regarded Jesus as righteous. God had upheld Jesus' cause against his enemies—including Paul's teachers and leaders.

The way Paul tells the story, it is not so much the case that Paul had made a personal decision for Christ. Rather, God had made a personal decision for Paul!

1. When has God broken in on your life to call for a realignment with his righteousness and his purposes?
2. When have you experienced God's direction so clearly that you had no need of consulting further with people?

THREE
Witnesses for the Defense

Galatians 1:18–24 ESV *Then after three years I went up to Jerusalem to visit Cephas and remained with him fifteen days. [19]But I saw none of the other apostles except James the Lord's brother. [20](In what I am writing to you, before God, I do not lie!) [21]Then I went into the regions of Syria and Cilicia. [22]And I was still unknown in person to the churches of Judea that are in Christ. [23]They only were hearing it said, "He who used to persecute us is now preaching the faith he once tried to destroy." [24]And they glorified God because of me.*

Key Observation. The Judean Christians found cause to praise God for the change in Paul's life.

Understanding the Word. A key to grasping the significance of Paul's narrative is the oath that he swears in the middle of the tale. Such oaths, calling God or the gods to witness, were frequently used in law courts to establish the truth of a statement. The oath essentially invites divine punishment if the speaker is lying. Why does Paul interject such an oath at this point? It seems that the rival teachers may have told Paul's converts a very different narrative. In this version of the story, Paul is both trained in the faith and commissioned as a missionary by the Jerusalem apostles. He ought to be teaching what the Jerusalem apostles want to see taught. This would include—so the rival teachers say—inviting Gentiles who trust Jesus also to join themselves to the covenant of Israel.

Paul is therefore trying to set the record straight in these paragraphs and calling God as a witness for the defense! God showed him very directly the new course his life needed to take when God showed Paul the resurrected Jesus. Paul understood his commission from God quite clearly and began to act on it immediately. It is known that he went up to Jerusalem on a few occasions. Paul must explain why he went and what he was looking for, if it was not because he was responsible to the Jerusalem apostles. He admits, then, that he went up to Jerusalem not too long after his conversion and call by God. But this happened a full three years later, after he had begun his missionary work. It happened, moreover, because Paul was taking the initiative to reach out to Peter. Peter is called "Cephas" here, the Aramaic version of his name.

(Both "Peter" and "Cephas" mean "rock.") Paul was acting collegially, seeking to make the acquaintance of a respected leader. He did *not* go up as a ministry candidate looking for the endorsement of an ordaining body! Indeed, the only other Jerusalem leader he met was James, one of the natural children of Mary and Joseph (see Mark 6:3).

After a mere two weeks' visit, Paul was off again to his work outside of Judea. Syria and Cilicia were the names of two Roman provincial regions. Syria was a region north of Galilee. Cilicia was the region that stretched northwest of Syria along the southeast coast of modern Turkey. Paul does not say explicitly what he was doing in the regions of Syria and Cilicia, just as he did not say what he had been doing in Arabia and Damascus. From the reports about Paul among the Judean churches, however, it is clear that he had been actively engaged in the mission to which God had called him. Paul seems most keen on emphasizing that he was not active as a missionary in Judea. The Judean Christians didn't know him by sight because he was not working under the authority or in the territory of the Jerusalem church. The reports that the Judean Christians were hearing about Paul's mission work, however, led them to conclude that God was behind the change. Paul effectively calls the Judean churches as witnesses for his own claim. If the persecutor is now the promoter, this is the Lord's doing!

1. What is the story of your own coming to faith and hearing God's call?
2. What consequences of your response to God's calling have given others reason to glorify God?

FOUR

Truth's Champion

Galatians 2:1–5 ESV *Then after fourteen years I went up again to Jerusalem with Barnabas, taking Titus along with me. [2]I went up because of a revelation and set before them (though privately before those who seemed influential) the gospel that I proclaim among the Gentiles, in order to make sure I was not running or had not run in vain. [3]But even Titus, who was with me, was not forced to be circumcised, though he was a Greek. [4]Yet because of false brothers secretly* *brought in—who slipped in to spy out our freedom that we have in Christ Jesus, so that they might bring us into slavery—*[5]*to them we did not yield in submission even for a moment, so that the truth of the gospel might be preserved for you.*

Key Observation. Paul worked hard to preserve the unity of the church without sacrificing the truth of the gospel.

Understanding the Word. Paul has been demonstrating that his message and his commission came by God's direct intervention. In this next episode, Paul claims that the leaders of the Jerusalem church recognize Paul's message and missionary practice to be valid. Because Paul cannot sacrifice the first point, he makes it clear that he made his second journey to Jerusalem at *God's* orders. He was not a lackey being summoned by his superiors.

Why does Paul fear that he may be working in vain? It is unlikely that he has doubts about his own message. It is more likely that he is concerned for the unity of the church's mission. Paul serves a vision for the church in which there is neither Jew nor Greek, since all are "one in Christ Jesus" (3:28). If he is not working in partnership with the Jerusalem apostles, however, the result will be far from unity.

We don't know why Paul and Barnabas took Titus along with them. Had he already become an important part of their ministry team? Did they want a Gentile Christian to be part of their delegation as a kind of Exhibit A? The important point for Paul is that Titus walked away from that meeting uncircumcised. Indeed, this point is so important that Paul jumps to it right away with no warning or preparation! If the Jerusalem apostles felt it necessary to correct Paul's message and practice, *that* would have been the time to do so. And if not Titus, then *no* Gentile Christian needed to be circumcised to be part of God's people in Christ.

The push for circumcising Titus wasn't coming from the Jerusalem apostles. Rather, it came from troublemakers pushing their way into conversations where they didn't belong. Paul calls these people "false brothers" (2 Cor. 11:26 ESV), though they would have no doubt regarded themselves as genuine believers. Indeed, they would have regarded themselves as champions of God's Law, much as Paul had been before his conversion. Therein lay the problem, however. They hadn't perceived what Paul saw so clearly in his *own* conversion. God was no longer defining his people by who followed the law of Moses. It wasn't necessary to become a practicing Jew to be part of God's people. It was necessary to be created anew by the Spirit into the likeness of God's Son, the Righteous One.

The images of slavery and freedom will run throughout Galatians. Paul himself looks back on life under the Torah as slavery under a harsh taskmaster. Experiencing Jesus' love and the Holy Spirit's guidance and empowerment was liberating for Paul. False brothers had tried to impose that slavery on Titus in Jerusalem. The rival teachers, by implication, are now seeking to impose slavery on the Gentile Christians in Galatia. Paul draws out another point of relevance for the Galatians. The "truth of the gospel" survived long enough to reach them thanks to Paul! This episode gives further proof that Paul is no people-pleaser. Rather, he has championed the truth of the gospel wherever this was jeopardized by others' short-sightedness.

1. How have you nurtured unity among Christians of different traditions where the truth of the gospel is not at stake? What further opportunities do you see?
2. When have you perceived the truth of the gospel to be in jeopardy? How did you respond?

FIVE

Further Witnesses for the Defense

Galatians 2:6–10 ESV *And from those who seemed to be influential (what they were makes no difference to me; God shows no partiality)—those, I say, who seemed influential added nothing to me. 7On the contrary, when they saw that I had been entrusted with the gospel to the uncircumcised, just as Peter had been entrusted with the gospel to the circumcised 8(for he who worked through Peter for his apostolic ministry to the circumcised worked also through me for mine to the Gentiles), 9and when James and Cephas and John, who seemed to be pillars, perceived the grace that was given to me, they gave the right hand of fellowship to Barnabas and me, that we should go to the Gentiles and they to the circumcised. 10Only, they asked us to remember the poor, the very thing I was eager to do.*

Key Observation. The results of Paul and Barnabas's mission demonstrated that God was actively at work in it and endorsed it.

Understanding the Word. Paul's eagerness to reach non-Jews reflects common expectations for what God would accomplish in the messianic age. Jews had long hoped that the nations around them would one day come to worship the one true God. This became one of the great works that the Messiah was expected to achieve. Paul quotes a number of Old Testament passages that fueled this hope in Romans 15:9–12.

What the Jerusalem leaders did *not* add to Paul's message and missionary work among Gentiles is extremely important for the situation in Galatia. Paul had presented the message that he proclaimed. He had no doubt laid out the lifestyle changes he required of his converts. It is highly likely that he, Barnabas, and Titus bore witness to the activity of God among the congregations that were forming. Paul will soon point the Galatians to their experience of the Holy Spirit as proof of God's acceptance (3:2–5). It stands to reason that he and his team would have offered this proof to Peter, James, and John as well. Indeed, precisely such results would have led the Jerusalem apostles to the conclusion that Paul said they had reached. They saw that God was working through Paul and Barnabas just as surely as God was working through Peter (also called "Cephas"). The result was that these leaders did not tell Paul that he needed to change anything that he was doing. God was obviously behind Paul's mission. Indeed, God had given Paul the grace—the gift and privilege—of this commissioning.

The two parties agree on some kind of division of labor, but the specifics are not quite clear. Is it strictly ethnic? Paul will continue to preach to Jews as well as Gentiles (see especially 1 Corinthians 9:20). Peter will preach to Gentiles as well as Jews, as his presence later in both Corinth and Rome suggest (1 Corinthians 1:12; 3:22). Did the division of labor fall by the wayside in the wake of the disagreement in Antioch (Gal. 2:11–14)? Perhaps the most significant aspect of the agreement is the mutual recognition it implied. God is at work in both missions, and this makes them partners and not rivals. We should note that Paul refers to Jews and Gentiles simply as "the circumcised" and "the uncircumcised" here. This operation is a major marker of ethnic identity for the Jewish people. Paul's mission poses a great stumbling block, for it calls into question the value of that identity in God's sight.

The Jerusalem apostles make one request of Paul—that he "should continue to remember the poor" (2:10 NIV). It is quite possible that Paul and Barnabas took relief funds with them on this visit (see Acts 11:27–30). It would be natural, then, to ask that Paul and Barnabas continue to do so as a symbol of their partnership. Indeed, Paul gives a great deal of attention to taking up a collection for the poor among the Judean churches throughout his mission fields. He is determined to prove faithful to this agreement and to his vision of a single, united church. The sharing of resources is a tangible sign of this spiritual reality (see Romans 15:25–31; 1 Corinthians 16:1–4; 2 Corinthians 8:1–9:15).

1. How does your church interact with other churches and missions to ensure partnership and effective division of labor?
2. How do you and your congregation continue to remember the poor? How far throughout the global church does your collective concern extend?

WEEK TWO

GATHERING DISCUSSION OUTLINE

A. **Open session in prayer.** Ask that God would astonish us anew with fresh insight from God's Word and transform us into the disciples that Jesus desires us to become.

B. **View the video for this week's readings.**

C. What were key insights or takeaways that you gained from your reading during the week and from watching the video commentary? In particular, how did these help you to grow in your faith and understanding of Scripture this week? What parts of the Bible lesson or study raised questions for you?

D. **Discuss selected questions from the daily readings.** Invite class members to share key insights or to raise questions that they found to be the most meaningful.

1. **KEY OBSERVATION:** Paul's gospel message has its roots in God's revealing to him who Jesus Christ really was—something no human being had been able to do.

   DISCUSSION QUESTION: How have other people, and how has God, contributed to opening your eyes to who Jesus Christ really is?

2. **KEY OBSERVATION:** When Paul was most on fire for the Law, he found himself most out of alignment with God's righteousness.

   DISCUSSION QUESTION: When has God broken in on your life to call for a realignment with his righteousness and his purposes?

3. **KEY OBSERVATION:** The Judean Christians found cause to praise God for the change in Paul's life.

   DISCUSSION QUESTION: What consequences of your response to God's calling have given others reason to glorify God?

4. **KEY OBSERVATION:** Paul worked hard to preserve the unity of the church without sacrificing the truth of the gospel.

   DISCUSSION QUESTION: How have you nurtured unity among Christians of different traditions where the truth of the gospel is not at stake? What further opportunities do you see?

5. **KEY OBSERVATION:** The results of Paul and Barnabas's mission demonstrated that God was actively at work in it and endorsed it.

   DISCUSSION QUESTION: How does your church interact with other churches and missions to ensure partnership and effective division of labor?

E. **As the study concludes, consider specific ways that this week's Bible lessons invite you to grow and call you to change.** How do they call us to think differently? How do they challenge us to change in order to align ourselves with God's work in the world? What specific actions should we take to apply the insights of the lesson into our daily lives? What kind of person does our Bible lesson call us to become?

F. **Close session with prayer.** Emphasize God's ongoing work of transformation in our lives in preparation for loving mission and service in the world. Pray for missing class members as well as for persons whom we need to invite to join our study.

WEEK THREE

Galatians 2:11–21

Gospel Truth

ONE

Who's at the Table?

Galatians 2:11–14 NIV *When Cephas came to Antioch, I opposed him to his face, because he stood condemned.* [12]*For before certain men came from James, he used to eat with the Gentiles. But when they arrived, he began to draw back and separate himself from the Gentiles because he was afraid of those who belonged to the circumcision group.* [13]*The other Jews joined him in his hypocrisy, so that by their hypocrisy even Barnabas was led astray.*

[14]*When I saw that they were not acting in line with the truth of the gospel, I said to Cephas in front of them all, "You are a Jew, yet you live like a Gentile and not like a Jew. How is it, then, that you force Gentiles to follow Jewish customs?"*

Key Observation. Christian community must reflect this gospel truth: the old categories that divide us no longer have value for people who are in Christ.

Understanding the Word. Paul presents his confrontation with Peter in Syrian Antioch as if the story is already familiar. The Galatians have probably heard about this episode before from the rival teachers. They could have told a version of this story that made Paul look like a renegade. In their version, the Jerusalem apostles and even Paul's coworker Barnabas came to understand that Gentile Christians remained *Gentiles* first. So Paul must now tell *his* version of the story to set the record straight.

Syrian Antioch was the hub of Paul and Barnabas's early mission work (see Acts 11:19–26; 13:1–3). In this cluster of house churches, Jewish believers did not treat the Gentile believers as Jews typically treated Gentiles. The Jews did not bring their own food. They did not place their food and drink on separate tables out of a concern that the Gentiles would pour offerings to other gods from their cups and thus defile the main table. They did not follow the typical practices that reminded everyone of the sharp boundaries that set them apart. Instead, Jewish and Gentile believers interacted quite freely and ate together at the same table. When Peter came to visit these congregations, he followed the local practice.

When stricter Jewish Christians (the "men . . . from James") showed up in Antioch, this all changed. They believed that the regulations of the Torah were still binding on Jewish believers in Jesus. The Torah was given to create a hedge around Israel. It protected Jews from the influence and idolatries of their Gentile neighbors. Peter ought to be setting an example of keeping the covenant, not relaxing the covenant, for Jewish believers in Jesus wherever he went! Peter yielded to the pressure. Soon all the Jewish Christians were being careful to gather only in Jewish Christian homes, where they could be assured that everything would be kosher. The new practice would also have affected the celebration of the Lord's Supper. Now there were essentially *two* Communion tables in Antioch, one for Jews and one for Gentiles.

Paul understands what Peter apparently did not. The change in practice has sent a clear message that the Gentile Christian is not as clean in God's sight as the Jewish Christian. It applies silent pressure to their Gentile brothers and sisters. If they want to be part of one church, it will have to be on *Jewish* Christian terms. The "truth that the gospel announces" (Gal. 2:14, author's translation) is at stake. The gospel expresses a new vision for human beings. The old categories that divide us no longer have value in the one body. As Paul will express later, "there is neither Jew nor Gentile" in this vision where all are in Christ and Christ is in all (3:28 NIV). In Antioch, Peter, Barnabas, and the other Jewish Christians stopped walking in the direction of this vision. Instead, they turned around toward the old vision for humanity in which there is still Jew and Gentile and an inviolable wall between the two.

Paul emphasizes that the change in practice was not a result of a change in convictions. He claims that Peter and Barnabas were simply putting on a show to please the representatives from James. Paul again shows himself unafraid to do the unpopular thing. He will *not* compromise the message to please human beings.

1. Who is welcome, and who is not welcome, at the Communion table in your church? Why or why not?
2. How does your congregation reflect the gospel truth that the old categories that divide us no longer have value for those who are in Christ? How does it not?

TWO

Falling in Line with the Divine

Galatians 2:15–16 NIV *"We who are Jews by birth and not sinful Gentiles [16]know that a person is not justified by the works of the law, but by faith in Jesus Christ. So we, too, have put our faith in Christ Jesus that we may be justified by faith in Christ and not by the works of the law, because by the works of the law no one will be justified."*

Key Observation. Trusting Jesus opens up the path to becoming righteous for Jew and Gentile alike.

Understanding the Word. Paul continues to write as if he is still addressing Peter and his fellow Jewish Christians in Syrian Antioch. He lays out what he believes to be the convictions he and Peter share and how Peter's behavior violated Peter's own convictions. At the same time, what he is writing has direct bearing also on what is happening in Galatia. The rival teachers, like the men from James, want to uphold the old boundaries around the Jewish people. They do not see, or are afraid to declare, that God has broken down those boundaries in his new outpouring of grace in Christ.

Paul calls into question the idea that he and Peter are still Jews and Gentiles first. If both Jews and Gentiles have come to recognize that they stand in the same need before God, do those old lines still have value? Is the Jew by birth really so different from the Gentile sinner? What really defines the Jew is doing what the Torah commanded. Peter, James, Paul, and Barnabas have all reached the same conclusion, however: doing what the Torah commands is not sufficient to stand righteous in God's sight. They have all agreed that trusting in Jesus, the Messiah, is indispensable. If "we Jews" understand that doing what the Torah commands (the "works of the law") isn't sufficient for us, what is the sense of imposing this way of life on Gentiles? It is enough that we, along with the Gentiles, hold together to what is indispensable. That is trusting Jesus and living into the new life that the Holy Spirit makes possible for both Jew and Gentile.

We might think of being justified here in terms of being lined up with a standard. We talk about justification in connection with lining up the left or right edges of a document we've typed. Paul is talking about two processes of transformation in these verses. In one process, I line myself up with the law of Moses and my life is transformed in the direction of reflecting its vision for human life. In the other process, I rely on the Spirit of Christ to align me with God's righteousness by aligning me with the mind and heart of Jesus. "Faith in Christ" means casting in my lot—and my eternal destiny—with the second process.

The problem with the law of Moses is not that it is impossible to live in line with it. Paul thought he himself had done a pretty good job. In Philippians he writes that, regarding righteousness as the Torah defines it, he was "blameless" (3:6). This does not mean that he kept the Torah perfectly. The Torah allows for the erasure of sins that are not the result of deliberate action. This is the purpose for many of the sacrifices and purifications it prescribes. The problem with the Torah is that it is not the final revelation of God's righteousness. *Jesus* is that revelation! God's resurrection of the condemned and crucified Jesus is God's dramatic declaration that Jesus is the Righteous One. Those who seek to align themselves with God's righteousness, therefore, can do no better than to align themselves with Jesus. The best assurance of acquittal at the judgment will be for God to recognize his righteous Son in each of the Son's followers.

1. Is Paul interested here in a verdict of not guilty on the day of judgment, a changed life that God approves as righteous, or both? Why do you think so?

2. In what ways has trusting Jesus moved you closer to living a life that God will approve as righteous since you first put your faith in Christ?

THREE
Letting Go of Old Lines

Galatians 2:17–18 NIV *"But if, in seeking to be justified in Christ, we Jews find ourselves also among the sinners, doesn't that mean that Christ promotes sin? Absolutely not!* [18]*If I rebuild what I destroyed, then I really would be a lawbreaker."*

Key Observation. Upholding lines of division between people who are in Christ sins against the Spirit's redrawing of lines *around* all people who are in Christ.

Understanding the Word. These can be difficult verses to understand until we remember the context. Paul is still speaking as if to Peter in Antioch in the wake of Peter's withdrawal from table fellowship with Gentile Christians. He is also still speaking from a *Jewish* Christian perspective, encouraging Peter to hold to his first convictions. Paul's argument in these two verses could be paraphrased in the following way.

"We are seeking to be righteous in God's sight by the path that trusting Jesus opened for us, just like our Gentile sisters and brothers. This leaves us in the same place as Gentiles, whom we Jews think of as straight-up 'sinners,' since they do not have God's law. So if we're now just 'sinners' alongside the Gentiles, has Jesus actually served *sin's* agenda? If we're not concerned to line up with the standards and regulations of the Torah any more, is Jesus advancing *sin's* interests rather than God's?"

Paul forcefully denies this conclusion. The Torah, which kept Jew and Gentile apart, no longer defines sinful or righteous behavior. The Holy Spirit has redrawn the lines between sinner and not sinner. The Holy Spirit descended upon Gentile and Jew alike as each came to trust in Jesus. What can be clearer proof that trusting Jesus is enough to make the Gentile clean in God's sight? I am only a sinner now (in the sense that matters) if I rebel against God's redrawing of these lines! Peter, Barnabas, and the other Jewish Christians in Antioch were indeed rebuilding what they destroyed. Under the Spirit's guidance Jewish and Gentile Christian are coming together in the one body. Under pressure of the people from James, the Jewish Christians were building up again the wall that kept Jew and Gentile separate. By acting as if those distinctions still mattered, they were dishonoring the Holy Spirit's work in the lives of both Jewish Christian and Gentile Christian.

Paul's emphatic denial that Christ promotes sin connects to a larger theme of Galatians as well. The goal of tearing down the walls that the Jewish law built around the people of God is not to allow people then to wander aimlessly. Much less is the goal to give them license to follow their self-centered impulses and desires. The goal is holiness of heart and life under the leading and the power of the Holy Spirit. Some Christians, in their desire to magnify grace and faith, teach a dangerous perversion of Paul's gospel. They will say that putting our faith in Jesus' death for us settles our eternal destiny then and there. Nothing I do after the hour I first believed affects that outcome. Such a view can make of Christ "a servant of sin," to use the language of Paul's Greek here more closely. It does not place enough weight on the change of life that Christ died to bring about in me. It does not place enough value on the life of righteousness that the *living* Christ seeks to live *through* me.

Paul will beg to differ with such a shallow version of the good news, as the remaining verses in this scripture will show.

1. What lines divide Christians from one another in your setting? How can you and your congregation move to nurture greater unity in the Spirit across those lines?
2. In what ways has Christ promoted your growth in holiness and righteousness?

FOUR

I'm Not Myself, Thank God!

Galatians 2:19–20 NIV *"For through the law I died to the law so that I might live for God.* [20]*I have been crucified with Christ and I no longer live, but Christ lives in me. The life I now live in the body, I live by faith in the Son of God, who loved me and gave himself for me."*

Key Observation. Christ has not accomplished the full purpose of his *death* for us until he has come *alive* within us and through us by the Holy Spirit.

Understanding the Word. Paul had found himself most hostile to God when he was most devoted to doing and enforcing the Torah. He had been sure that the way to align himself with God's righteousness was by lining his life up with the commandments in the law of Moses. That path, however, left him dead to what God was doing in Israel's midst on behalf of the world. He found himself every bit as much God's enemy as any Gentile sinner. The law of Moses, which did not help Paul line up with God's righteousness after all, will not help the Gentiles do so either. And so Paul had to die to what he was in order to become what God wished to make of him. This included dying *to* the Law, which Paul hints here was ultimately in line with God's purposes *for* the Law and revealed *in* the Law. This is far from obvious, so Paul will give a lot of attention in chapters 3 and 4 to tracing out how this works.

Paul also found himself reconciled to God in the same way that any Gentile sinner would be reconciled to God. This was through an encounter with the living Christ that awakened trust in Jesus and all that Jesus' dying for him had won for him. Of course this included forgiveness of his past sins—most starkly his hostility against Jesus' followers! It also included a share in the Holy Spirit, as Paul will go on to emphasize later in this letter.

This brings Paul to what is perhaps his clearest and most beautiful expression of the Christian life. Paul has "come alive to God" in a way he had never known before. And this coming alive has happened for him because Christ is coming alive *in him*. Notice the reciprocity implicit in this description. Jesus loves me and gave his life for me, to bring me back to God the Father and secure for me the Holy Spirit. Now I give what remains of my life to Jesus, for him to live through me. Christ's giving of himself becomes the focal act that defines my responses in every situation. All of life comes to be lived with a view to giving oneself over to Christ, to his interests, and to his agenda.

It is a death to the Law, but it is also a death to one's own ego. The "I" no longer drives my life in the body. Christ drives and directs my life in the body by his indwelling Spirit. Paul will speak elsewhere of the "old person" (Col. 3:9; Eph. 4:22) and of the flesh with its cravings and desires (see Galatians 5:17). By dying with Christ, we are given the opportunity to die to all of this so that something new can be born and come to life in us. This is the new person that the Spirit creates in us, that shows God the obedience that God deserves, that reflects the heart and character of the Son. Paul will also refer to this as a "new creation," which is all that matters now in God's sight (6:15). Being circumcised can add nothing to this and remaining uncircumcised can take nothing away. There is no surer path to righteousness than this—for God's Righteous One to take over and come alive in me.

1. What about your life right now reflects Christ alive in and living through you? In what ways is the Spirit leading you to die a little more to your ego and give more room to Christ?
2. How much of your life, day by day, is shaped in response to the love Christ showed you in giving himself for you?

FIVE

Displacing Grace Would Be a Disgrace

Galatians 2:21 NIV *"I do not set aside the grace of God, for if righteousness could be gained through the law, Christ died for nothing!"*

Key Observation. The value *we* place on living the new life Christ has made possible for us should match the value *Christ* placed on securing it for us.

Understanding the Word. We tend to encounter the word *grace* only in religious contexts, usually Christian contexts. It has become a church word. Paul and his audience, however, encountered the word in many settings. Theirs is a world that utterly depends on grace—on the goodwill, favor, and generosity of those who are better off to help those who are less well off. Theirs is also a world that clearly understood that grace ("favor") had to be met with grace ("gratitude"). Someone is offering me the help or the resources that I desire or need. If I accept the gift, I also accept a personal obligation to the giver. I enter into a grace relationship in which I will show honor and loyalty to the person who has helped me, and I will seek for any opportunity to render service in return. Even though grace is not a *religious* word, it is still a *sacred* obligation.

Paul has just given eloquent expression to the proportions of God's gift and favor in 2:19–20. It may be useful to note that Paul believes *Christ's* giving of himself to be fully an act of *God's* generosity toward us. Christ does not give himself over to a tortured and bloody death to appease an angry God. Christ's death is the demonstration of *God's* outreaching love and favor toward *us*. Would anyone throw away such a gift? Everyone in Paul's audience shudders at the thought of responding to such grace so disgracefully. And yet this is precisely what Paul claims his converts are about to do if they remove themselves from the Spirit's care and place themselves under the care of the Law instead.

The NIV offers a better translation of this verse than the NRSV. The NRSV reads, "if justification comes through the law, then Christ died for nothing." *Justification* is a pretty loaded theological word with a lot of baggage. What's relevant here, though, is that Paul does *not* use that word. He's talking about attaining "righteousness," a quality of character and action that God approves. The implication of saying that righteousness doesn't come through the Law is clear. Righteousness *does* come through trusting Jesus and through all that trust opens up for the believer. Righteousness is what Paul hopes he and all his converts will attain together: "Through the Spirit we eagerly await by faith the righteousness for which we hope" (5:5 NIV). Paul will give a great deal of attention to how the Spirit guides and empowers us to walk in righteousness before God (5:13–6:10).

As we review this week's readings, we find Paul telling us quite clearly what we should expect from God in response to our believing. Paul does *not* say that we should expect God to pour out material blessings on us. He does *not* say that we should expect God to give us a life free from pain and trial. He *does* say that we should expect God to be at work in our lives to make us more like Jesus. We should expect God to expand our capacity for love and service, to change our focus from advancing our own interests to advancing the good of others.

1. How can remembering the love and favor Christ has shown you help you respond to some challenge in a manner more likely to please God?
2. How has your life been shaped to this point by gratitude toward God? What would change if gratitude were to shape your life more fully?

WEEK THREE

GATHERING DISCUSSION OUTLINE

A. **Open session in prayer.** Ask that God would astonish us anew with fresh insight from God's Word and transform us into the disciples that Jesus desires us to become.

B. **View the video for this week's readings.**

C. What were key insights or takeaways that you gained from your reading during the week and from watching the video commentary? In particular, how did these help you to grow in your faith and understanding of Scripture this week? What parts of the Bible lesson or study raised questions for you?

D. **Discuss selected questions from the daily readings.** Invite class members to share key insights or to raise questions that they found to be the most meaningful.

1. **KEY OBSERVATION:** Christian community must reflect this gospel truth: the old categories that divide us no longer have value for people who are in Christ.

   DISCUSSION QUESTION: How does your congregation reflect the gospel truth that the old categories that divide us no longer have value for those who are in Christ? How does it not?

2. **KEY OBSERVATION:** Trusting Jesus opens up the path to becoming righteous for Jew and Gentile alike.

DISCUSSION QUESTION: In what ways has trusting Jesus moved you closer to living a life that God will approve as righteous since you first put your faith in Christ?

3. **KEY OBSERVATION:** Upholding lines of division between people who are in Christ sins against the Spirit's redrawing of lines *around* all people who are in Christ.

   DISCUSSION QUESTION: What lines divide Christians from one another in your setting? How can you and your congregation move to nurture greater unity in the Spirit across those lines?

4. **KEY OBSERVATION:** Christ has not accomplished the full purpose of his *death* for us until he has come *alive* within us and through us by the Holy Spirit.

   DISCUSSION QUESTION: What about your life right now reflects Christ alive in and living through you? In what ways is the Spirit leading you to die a little more to your ego and give more room to Christ?

5. **KEY OBSERVATION:** The value *we* place on living the new life Christ has made possible for us should match the value *Christ* placed on securing it for us.

   DISCUSSION QUESTION: How has your life been shaped to this point by gratitude toward God? What would change if gratitude were to shape your life more fully?

E. **As the study concludes, consider specific ways that this week's Bible lessons invite you to grow and call you to change.** How do they call us to think differently? How do they challenge us to change in order to align ourselves with God's work in the world? What specific actions should we take to apply the insights of the lesson into our daily lives? What kind of person does our Bible lesson call us to become?

F. **Close session with prayer.** Emphasize God's ongoing work of transformation in our lives in preparation for loving mission and service in the world. Pray for missing class members as well as for persons whom we need to invite to join our study.

WEEK FOUR

Galatians 3:1–22

The Law and the Promise

ONE

All the Evidence You Need

Galatians 3:1–5 *You foolish Galatians! Who has bewitched you? It was before your eyes that Jesus Christ was publicly exhibited as crucified! [2]The only thing I want to learn from you is this: Did you receive the Spirit by doing the works of the law or by believing what you heard? [3]Are you so foolish? Having started with the Spirit, are you now ending with the flesh? [4]Did you experience so much for nothing?—if it really was for nothing. [5]Well then, does God supply you with the Spirit and work miracles among you by your doing the works of the law, or by your believing what you heard?*

Key Observation. By trusting Jesus, the Galatians received God's Holy Spirit. The Spirit who started them on their journey of transformation will see them through to the end.

Understanding the Word. This week we begin to encounter the arguments that Paul gives the Galatians for rejecting the rival teachers' advice. Paul opens with his strongest one. If he can gain their assent to this one point, he will have already won his case. But first he gets their attention by scolding them. He reminds the Galatians that he had presented Jesus Christ to them quite openly as crucified. The force of this comes from the preceding verse. The immense price Jesus paid for their redemption is the "grace of God" that, Paul claims, they are in danger of brushing off! The extreme sacrifice that Jesus made on their behalf is the death that they are about to render useless where they're concerned! Have the rival teachers been using dark magic to cloud the minds of the Galatians? What else could account for their losing sight of what had been so clear?

The decisive question is this: What opened you up to the experience of God's Holy Spirit? The Galatians would not have to wonder. When the Holy Spirit fell upon an early Christian congregation, it was obvious. It was an undeniable experience of God's marvelous power and presence. And they would have to admit that they enjoyed a share in God's Holy Spirit purely as a result of trusting in Jesus' death and resurrection on their behalf.

This passage points us to the importance of the experience of the Holy Spirit in Paul's mission and Paul's churches. Paul understands the coming of the Holy Spirit to fulfill God's promise to Abraham to bless all the nations. Paul might have looked to the book of Ezekiel for confirmation of his conviction. In Ezekiel, God promises to pour "a new spirit" into God's people. This spirit will empower them to do what is righteous in God's sight and so experience God's blessings (11:19–20; 36:26–27). The fact that the Galatians have received the Holy Spirit gave absolute proof that God had adopted them into the family of blessing (Gal. 3:13–14; 4:6–7). They are not still outside of the family, as the rival teachers assert. Indeed, they have already inherited!

The rival teachers would have presented accepting circumcision and the Torah-observant lifestyle as a step forward. "If you want to make progress in virtue and discipleship, the law of Moses is a perfect exercise program for you." Paul respects the desire to make progress in discipleship. But moving from a focus on the Spirit to a focus on the flesh (here, specifically cutting the flesh of the foreskin) is not progress! A candle cannot add to the brightness of the sun! Indeed, if the Galatians turned to the Law at this point, they would be denying the value of the gifts they had already received. Their experience of the Holy Spirit would prove to be "for nothing" (3:4).

Knowing the truth and making it known is indeed important. But we also cannot neglect *experiencing* the Holy One in our midst. If the Holy Spirit is not present and active in our lives, we lack the promised inheritance (3:14). We lack the Partner and the Power that will see us through to the end of our journey of transformation (5:5–6).

1. What has been your own experience of the Holy Spirit's active presence in your life and your faith community?
2. To what extent have your faith communities nurtured an awareness of and dependence upon the Holy Spirit?

TWO

The Essential Family Resemblance

Galatians 3:6–9 *Just as Abraham "believed God, and it was reckoned to him as righteousness," [7]so, you see, those who believe are the descendants of Abraham. [8]And the scripture, foreseeing that God would justify the Gentiles by faith, declared the gospel beforehand to Abraham, saying, "All the Gentiles shall be blessed in you." [9]For this reason, those who believe are blessed with Abraham who believed.*

Key Observation. The genuine children of Abraham share his trust in God's promise and power.

Understanding the Word. Who is a part of Abraham's family and, therefore, an heir of God's promises? Paul assures the Gentile Galatian Christians several times that they have *already* become Abraham's sons and daughters (3:7, 29; 4:28, 31). It is clearly important to them to know that they are part of Abraham's family. Why give so much attention to this question?

The rival teachers may have been the first to emphasize the importance of becoming part of Abraham's family. Only Abraham and his proper offspring are heirs of God's promises. Circumcision has always been the essential mark of belonging to Abraham's family. Abraham received that mark in his own flesh, as did every male member of his household. Indeed, anyone who was not circumcised would not remain in the family (see Genesis 17:9–14). Two hundred years before Paul, a Jewish teacher in Jerusalem remembered Abraham's story in this way. Abraham "kept the law of the Most High," received circumcision, and was faithful when tested. *In response to all this,* God gave Abraham his great promises (Sirach 44:19–21). Paul sees the story quite differently. God promised, and Abraham trusted and walked forward in line with that trust.

In the NRSV, Galatians 3:6 begins a new paragraph. This verse, however, really completes the thought of 3:5. What was true for Abraham will be true for all of Abraham's children. The Galatians received the Spirit by trusting "just as Abraham 'trusted God, and it was credited to him as righteousness'" (author's translation). Paul recites Genesis 15:6 here almost word for word. This text significantly appears two full chapters earlier in Genesis than the account of Abraham receiving circumcision.

How can one spot the genuine children of Abraham? The fundamental mark of family resemblance is faith. It is not the condition of the foreskin. As Paul understands Abraham's story, it was trust that characterized Abraham. And those who share that fundamental characteristic are Abraham's children. Trust in God is the essential Abrahamic gene. The promise that Abraham believed in Genesis 15:6 was that God would give him countless descendants. Paul sees God fulfilling this promise as the proclamation of the gospel awakens the faith gene in people from all nations.

Paul suggests that this was God's plan from the beginning. He recalls another promise God made to Abraham: "all the nations of the earth shall be blessed in [you]" (Gen. 18:18). The NRSV reads "all the Gentiles" (Gal. 3:8), but the phrase "all the nations" typically includes both the Jewish and the Gentile nations. Paul hears this as a preannouncement of the gospel. He connects this promise with his conviction that "God would align the Gentiles with his righteousness by faith" (Gal. 3:8, author's translation).

As the "father of many nations" (Rom. 4:18), Abraham could not be the spiritual father only of those people who lived like Jews, as the rival teachers are preaching. The law of Moses is for *one* nation—and works specifically to create boundaries between that one nation and every other nation. It could not be the vehicle by which God would create one family for Abraham out of *every* nation. The Holy Spirit, to which all had access by trusting Jesus, will be this agent.

1. How are you participating in extending the blessing for "all the nations" to the unreached in many of those nations?

2. What do you know of Abraham's story? How did his trust in God's promises transform his life and guide his actions?

THREE
Trading Blessing for Curse?

Galatians 3:10–14 *For all who rely on the works of the law are under a curse; for it is written, "Cursed is everyone who does not observe and obey all the things written in the book of the law."* [11]*Now it is evident that no one is justified before God by the law; for "The one who is righteous will live by faith."* [12]*But the law does not rest on faith; on the contrary, "Whoever does the works of the law will live by them."* [13]*Christ redeemed us from the curse of the law by becoming a curse for us—for it is written, "Cursed is everyone who hangs on a tree"—*[14]*in order that in Christ Jesus the blessing of Abraham might come to the Gentiles, so that we might receive the promise of the Spirit through faith.*

Key Observation. The death of Jesus brought an end to the Law's authority and power to curse, releasing the promised Holy Spirit in its place.

Understanding the Word. Paul has been developing a contrast between trusting and doing the Law (2:15–16; 3:2–5). In yesterday's passage, Paul turned to the example of Abraham to develop the connection between trust and the experience of blessing. Now he completes the contrast by connecting "works of the law" with living under the threat of a curse. This is a dense paragraph that needs careful unpacking.

Paul quotes Deuteronomy 27:26 as proof that a curse hangs over the head of everyone who enters the covenant of the Torah. (And who would choose to live in fear of the curse rather than remain in a life of blessing?) This was, in fact, the last of twelve curses pronounced over the Israelites as they renewed the covenant before Moses' death. Indeed, for much of its history, Israel lived not merely in *fear* of the curse but *experiencing* the curse. By Paul's time, Israel had spent more time as the possession of Gentile empires than as an independent kingdom. Jews had been scattered throughout the Mediterranean and the Middle East. These were all facets of the curses that Deuteronomy promised a disobedient people.

Paul introduces another scripture as evidence that the Law is *not* the path to righteousness. According to Habakkuk 2:4, "the righteous person will live on the basis of trust" (author's translation). The verse closely associates "righteousness" with "trust." This reinforces Paul's lesson from Abraham, who "trusted God, and it was accounted to him as righteousness" (Gal. 3:6, author's translation). Another quotation from Scripture shows that the Law is *not* linked with trust. Rather, "the one who does these things will live through them" (Lev. 18:4–5, author's translation). Paul is intent on driving this wedge between faith and the Law to refute the rival teachers. They have been promoting the Law as the natural complement to, and completion of, trusting Jesus. Paul, therefore, must show the Law to be incompatible with trusting Jesus.

Paul then connects Jesus' death with the curse that the Law threatens. He finds in Deuteronomy 21:23 the claim that anyone left hanging on a tree is cursed. The point of this statement is to limit the amount of time an executed criminal is left exposed. For Paul, however, the greater point is that Christ willingly suffered an accursed death in order to redeem people from the Law's curse. He brought the term of the Law to an end by buying out all the people under its power. This leads Paul to his climax. In this way, Jesus has secured for everyone who trusts him the blessing that was promised in Abraham. This blessing is the Holy Spirit, poured out upon Jewish and Gentile believer alike to make both righteous.

By claiming that Christ redeemed us from the Torah's curse, Paul shows that the Torah now belongs to the past. It is not a way forward for anyone. The present time is meant for something else—for walking in line with the Spirit (see 5:25). Choosing to put oneself under the Law now on this side of Jesus' death would also make a mockery of that death. Jesus' death (accursed!) was the price of liberation. Returning oneself to slavery after the fact nullifies that costly gift and its achievement. It amounts to setting aside God's gift (2:21).

1. How do Paul's words here affect how you apply Old Testament rules to your life (for example, tithing, a particular day of rest)?
2. Do you feel more as one living under the threat of a curse or as one experiencing freedom and blessing in your walk with God? Why?

FOUR
Read the Fine Print

Galatians 3:15–18 *Brothers and sisters, I give an example from daily life: once a person's will has been ratified, no one adds to it or annuls it. [16]Now the promises were made to Abraham and to his offspring; it does not say, "And to offsprings," as of many; but it says, "And to your offspring," that is, to one person, who is Christ. [17]My point is this: the law, which came four hundred thirty years later, does not annul a covenant previously ratified by God, so as to nullify the promise. [18]For if the inheritance comes from the law, it no longer comes from the promise; but God granted it to Abraham through the promise.*

Key Observation. The period of the Law's jurisdiction is just a great parenthesis in God's history of salvation. The promise to Abraham and its fulfillment in connection with Christ are the main events.

Understanding the Word. A picture of the role of the Torah in God's plan for humanity is beginning to emerge in this chapter. God's promise to Abraham is eclipsing Moses' giving of the Law. Living under the Law looks more like a condition that needed remedying rather than broadening. Jesus' death provides ransom from that condition so that the promise made to Abraham can flood all nations, Jewish and Gentile. Paul now reaches for an analogy from everyday legal practice to sharpen the focus.

Paul's audience would have been very familiar with making wills. Providing for the distribution of one's property after one's death was an ancient concern. There were variations between Roman law, the laws in Greek cities, and native practices. Nevertheless, it was essentially a given that a will would be respected. Once it was properly ratified, its provisions had to be executed. Other agreements made with other parties could not alter or encumber the will. This is the frame of reference Paul wants his hearers to have in mind.

When God made his promises to Abraham, he was essentially setting up an inheritance. And, Paul says, if you look closely at the language—as one should with legal documents!—the inheritance is given to Abraham "and to [his] seed" (NIV). Singular. Paul knows, as would his audience, that the singular word "offspring" or "seed" can refer to one specific descendant or to a whole group of descendants. Paul suggests that the singular form of the word here points to a singular person—Christ! God's bequest belongs to him and to whomever *he* chooses to give a share. And the giving of the Law to the people of Israel does not alter this bequest.

The number 430 is a good biblical number. It come from Exodus 12:40, where the length of time that the Hebrews lived in Egypt is given as 430 years. The time from Abraham to the giving of the Law at Sinai would have been longer, but this number is enough to make the point. The (much later) law of Moses is not an addendum to be tacked onto the bequest God made to Abraham for the benefit of all the nations. It is an entirely unrelated arrangement. For the rival teachers to claim otherwise is to challenge the validity of God's will.

God bequeathed this promise only to Abraham and to one specific offspring of Abraham, namely Jesus. How, then, is the promise of "many descendants" fulfilled? How do the promised blessings reach the many? The answer will come just a few paragraphs later. People become descendants of Abraham and heirs of the promise by joining themselves to the one Seed. As Jews and Gentiles, slaves, and free persons, men and women are baptized into Christ, they all become one with Christ. They become "Abraham's seed" themselves (Gal. 3:27–29 NIV). Notice the stunning claim here. Even Jews are not "Abraham's seed" by virtue of natural descent from Abraham. Gentiles do not join "Abraham's seed" by joining the Jewish people through circumcision and law observance. Jew and Gentile alike become "Abraham's seed" as each trusts in Christ and is plunged (immersed, baptized) into Christ. Paul will lead out these implications explicitly in his reading of the stories of Hagar and Sarah (4:21–31).

1. Why does Paul place such a great emphasis on God's promise to Abraham as the foundation for deliverance?
2. How does Paul's view of God's overarching plan for making all things right give a more exalted role to Christ than the rival teachers' view?

FIVE
The Big Question

Galatians 3:19–22 *Why then the law? It was added because of transgressions, until the offspring would come to whom the promise had been made; and it was ordained through angels by a mediator.* [20]*Now a mediator involves more than one party; but God is one.*

[21]*Is the law then opposed to the promises of God? Certainly not! For if a law had been given that could make alive, then righteousness would indeed come through the law.* [22]*But the scripture has imprisoned all things under the power of sin, so that what was promised through faith in Jesus Christ might be given to those who believe.*

Key Observation. The Law played a purposeful role in God's plan, but the promise reflects more clearly the oneness of the God of both Jews and Gentiles.

Understanding the Word. What, then, *is* the role of the Torah in God's overall plan for restoring humanity, if it is not what the rival teachers claim? Paul raises this question but doesn't give much of an answer yet. Indeed, the bulk of *this* paragraph is still aimed at demonstrating the limitations on and inferiority of the Law.

Paul says cryptically that the Law was given "because of transgressions" or "for the sake of transgressions." This terse phrase could be understood in any one of four ways: (1) the Law limits or restrains transgressions; (2) the Law provides mechanisms for dealing with transgressions, such as sacrifices; (3) the Law *provokes* transgressions; or (4) the Law identifies what actions *are* transgressions. It is not immediately clear which sense Paul has in mind here. He will shortly go on to speak of the Law's role in more detail in a way that suggests that he has the first meaning in mind (3:23–25). (In Romans, he will later suggest the third and fourth possibilities.) What *is* clear from 3:19 is, again, the temporary role of the Law in God's plan. Paul says once more that the Law was "added," reminding us of the model of 3:15–18. And it was put in place only "until" the coming of the Seed, who is Christ. The expiration date for the Law's force is already decades past by the time Paul writes Galatians.

God gave his promises to Abraham directly. The Law was given through a series of middlemen. We are familiar with Moses' role as a mediator (see Exodus 20:18–22a). We may be surprised to hear Paul speak of *angels* as another link in the chain. Exodus doesn't give any hint of their involvement, but Jewish traditions arose that introduce them into the story. This is reflected also in Acts 7:38, 53 and Hebrews 2:2. Paul thinks that this is another reason that the Law is inferior to the promise. He associates the promise with the fundamental creed of Judaism: "Hear, O Israel: The LORD our God, the LORD is one" (Deut. 6:4 NIV). Pious Jews recited this text twice daily, declaring the uniqueness of the one God in the midst of Gentiles who worshiped their many gods. Paul's logic is a bit loose, but his point is profound. The Law was all about setting the Jewish people apart from Gentiles as holy to the Lord. The promise in Christ is all about the one God gathering Jews and Gentiles into one redeemed body (see Galatians 3:27–28). As Paul will make clearer in Romans, the God of the Jews must also be the God of the Gentiles, "since God is one" (Rom. 3:30).

The Law had a purposeful role to play. The problem only emerges when trying to make of the Law something that it is *not* in God's larger purposes for humanity. The Law is only against God's promises where it is promoted as an alternative means to attain those promises. If the Law could make all people come alive to God, it would be the means by which to attain righteousness (see Galatians 3:21). Paul's own experience, however, drove home for him the conviction that this was not the case. It was only in *dying* to the Law that Paul came alive to God (2:19).

1. What helps to restrain your own impulses to sin, if the Law is no longer what regulates your life?
2. What walls of division in the body of Christ still need to be torn down so that we better reflect the oneness of God?

WEEK FOUR

GATHERING DISCUSSION OUTLINE

A. **Open session in prayer.** Ask that God would astonish us anew with fresh insight from God's Word and transform us into the disciples that Jesus desires us to become.

B. **View the video for this week's readings.**

C. What were key insights or takeaways that you gained from your reading during the week and from watching the video commentary? In particular, how did these help you to grow in your faith and understanding of Scripture this week? What parts of the Bible lesson or study raised questions for you?

D. **Discuss selected questions from the daily readings.** Invite class members to share key insights or to raise questions that they found to be the most meaningful.

1. **KEY OBSERVATION:** By trusting Jesus, the Galatians received God's Holy Spirit. The Spirit who started them on their journey of transformation will see them through to the end.

   DISCUSSION QUESTION: What has been your own experience of the Holy Spirit's active presence in your life and your faith community?

2. **KEY OBSERVATION:** The genuine children of Abraham share his trust in God's promise and power.

   DISCUSSION QUESTION: How are you participating in extending the blessing for "all the nations" to the unreached in many of those nations?

3. **KEY OBSERVATION:** The death of Jesus brought an end to the Law's authority and power to curse, releasing the promised Holy Spirit in its place.

   DISCUSSION QUESTION: How do Paul's words here affect how you apply Old Testament rules to your life (for example, tithing, a particular day of rest)?

4. **KEY OBSERVATION:** The period of the Law's jurisdiction is just a great parenthesis in God's history of salvation. The promise to Abraham and its fulfillment in connection with Christ are the main events.

   DISCUSSION QUESTION: How does Paul's view of God's overarching plan for making all things right give a more exalted role to Christ than the rival teachers' view?

5. **KEY OBSERVATION:** The Law played a purposeful role in God's plan, but the promise reflects more clearly the oneness of the God of both Jews and Gentiles.

   DISCUSSION QUESTION: What helps to restrain your own impulses to sin, if the Law is no longer what regulates your life?

E. **As the study concludes, consider specific ways that this week's Bible lessons invite you to grow and call you to change.** How do they call us to think differently? How do they challenge us to change in order to align ourselves with God's work in the world? What specific actions should we take to apply the insights of the lesson into our daily lives? What kind of person does our Bible lesson call us to become?

F. **Close session with prayer.** Emphasize God's ongoing work of transformation in our lives in preparation for loving mission and service in the world. Pray for missing class members as well as for persons whom we need to invite to join our study.

WEEK FIVE

Galatians 3:23–4:20

No Turning Back the Clock

ONE

Humanity Comes of Age

Galatians 3:23–25 ESV *Now before faith came, we were held captive under the law, imprisoned until the coming faith would be revealed. [24]So then, the law was our guardian until Christ came, in order that we might be justified by faith. [25]But now that faith has come, we are no longer under a guardian, . . .*

Key Observation. The law of Moses ensured that the seedbed of Israel would be securely in place when the Seed, Christ, finally came into the world.

Understanding the Word. Paul continues to paint an unflattering picture of life under the Law. It kept people under guard, hemming them in on this side and that. There was actually a great deal of overlap here with the kind of picture that Jews who appreciated living under the Law might paint. An anonymous Jew wrote a book called *The Letter of Aristeas* in the second or first century before Christ. In this book, a high priest explains the Torah and its purpose to some Gentile visitors. "Our lawgiver . . . built strong fences and iron walls around us so that we might not mix with people of other nations. He wanted to keep us pure in body and soul, free from empty thoughts, worshiping the one and only God. To keep us from being corrupted, he hedged us on every side with purity laws and rules about what we could and could not eat or touch."[2]

---

2. *Letter of Aristeas*, 139, 142, author's translation.

For this author, the law of Moses was a strong and welcome defense against the errors of the Gentiles.

Paul finds a good analogy for the Torah, its role, and its term limits in the figure of the pedagogue (in the English Standard Version [ESV], "guardian"). This figure would have been quite familiar to the Galatians, even if they never had a pedagogue themselves. They would have seen pedagogues leading the young sons from families of more-than-moderate means around their cities. They would have seen pedagogues lampooned in comedies in their theaters. The pedagogue was a household slave who was particularly charged with taking care of male children from about the age of six through their coming of age. He would keep the child safe, teach manners, ensure that homework was done, and apply discipline as needed. He was often portrayed as a strict tyrant, but he protected a boy from bad influences and from the boy's own inclinations. When the child came of age, however, he was no longer under the pedagogue's authority.

The Law had a positive, but temporary, function. God set it in place to provide protective discipline for the people of Israel, from whom the promised Seed was to come. John Chrysostom, a fourth-century Christian preacher, captured the Law's positive role in this way: "If the Law had not been given, sin would have wrecked everything and everyone. There would not have been any Jews to *listen* to Christ in the first place."[3] The Law preserved the seedbed, but the Seed had now already come.

The rival teachers were trying to keep the covenant of the Law in force after the coming of the Seed. To do so meant using the Law in a way that was contrary to God's purpose for it. It meant acting as if the great "coming of age" in Jesus' death and resurrection and in the giving of the Spirit never happened. It was essentially an act of defiance against God's authority to order the times. The Law had to yield to the greater way that God had prepared to bring *all* people, and not just *one* people, in line with God's righteousness. If maintained, the walls that once served to protect would now only serve as a prison.

---

3. Commentary on Galatians 3:22; John Chrysostom, ed. Philip Schaff, "Homilies on Galatians," in *Homilies on Galatians, Ephesians, Philippians, Colossians, Thessalonians, Timothy, Titus, and Philemon*, NPNF series 1, vol. 13 (Edinburgh: T & T Clark, 1889), 29.

1. How does Paul's view of the Law's role in Israel's life and in God's plan orient you to reading and valuing the Old Testament?
2. What is our relationship to the Old Testament as moral law according to Paul in this letter?

TWO

One New Humanity in the One New Man

Galatians 3:26–29 ESV . . . *for in Christ Jesus you are all sons of God, through faith. [27]For as many of you as were baptized into Christ have put on Christ. [28]There is neither Jew nor Greek, there is neither slave nor free, there is no male and female, for you are all one in Christ Jesus. [29]And if you are Christ's, then you are Abraham's offspring, heirs according to promise.*

Key Observation. How society has taught us to categorize, limit, and relate to one another must have no force among those who are "in Christ."

Understanding the Word. Old Testament texts like Exodus 4:22–23 and Deuteronomy 14:1–2 applied the title "sons" or "children of God" to the people of Israel. Paul applies the title to *all* people who are "in Christ," whether Israelites or Gentiles. Where Jews and Gentiles are "in Christ" together, there is no longer a "Jew" over here and a "Gentile" over there. There are only people "in Christ." Trying to introduce the Law at this point means reintroducing the division of people into Jews and Gentiles. It means undoing what God has done.

Paul recalls the ritual of baptism to drive this home. In the early church, people were often baptized by being fully immersed in water. This became a powerful image that could be developed in several ways. In Romans, Paul will speak of being submerged in baptism as the burial of a believer's old self with Christ. What burst forth from the water is a new person, living a new life of righteousness with Christ. Here, Paul speaks of being submerged into the water of baptism as being plunged into Christ. The person goes in a Jew or Gentile, a slave or a free person, a male or a female. The believer emerges, however, with Christ engulfing, covering, and enveloping him or her like a garment. After baptism, what we should see when we look at one another is Christ, into whom we have all been plunged together.

The Jew divided up humanity into Jew and Gentile, slave and free person, male and female. The Greek would replace the first pair with "Greek and barbarian" (cf. Colossians 3:9–11), a Roman with "Roman and non-Roman." All would affirm the second and third pairs to be meaningful. These divisions of humanity are not just innocent observations of difference. The distinctions are laden with value judgments and unequal power relations. They reflect the racism and chauvinism of this "present evil age" from which Christ rescued us (1:4), not the new creation.

Paul's vision challenges us to break fully free from the power of this "present evil age" on our relationships and roles within the church and our outreach beyond. Paul would challenge a Christian named Philemon in this regard. Onesimus had left Philemon as Philemon's slave. After spending some time with Paul, Onesimus put his trust in Jesus and received baptism. Would Philemon still cling to the old relationship, according to which he (a free man) owned a slave? Or would Philemon honor the new relationship, according to which he and Onesimus had become brothers together in God's family? (see Philemon 1:8–21). Living as new creation requires living in very new ways with one another.

Paul concludes this paragraph returning to the topics of 3:15–18. Those who have been baptized into Christ have become part of Christ. They have thereby become part of the singular Seed, the one descendant of Abraham, to whom the promises were given. By virtue of being one with the Seed, they have become heirs of the promises themselves. There is nothing more that circumcision or Torah observance can do for them—except *undo* what the Spirit has already accomplished in their midst.

1. What would need to change in your church for it to reflect fully Paul's vision for oneness in Christ?

2. Into what pairs of categories have you been taught to partition people? How do these categories interfere with loving your Christian sister or brother as yourself?

THREE
Slaves to the Way Things Work

Galatians 4:1–5 ESV *I mean that the heir, as long as he is a child, is no different from a slave, though he is the owner of everything, [2]but he is under guardians and managers until the date set by his father. [3]In the same way we also, when we were children, were enslaved to the elementary principles of the world. [4]But when the fullness of time had come, God sent forth his Son, born of woman, born under the law, [5]to redeem those who were under the law, so that we might receive adoption as sons.*

Key Observation. Christ sets us free from running in the ruts society has dug out for us to make us live out our lives perpetuating its systems and values.

Understanding the Word. Paul returns to the analogy of minor children growing up in the household and coming of age. He shifts the frame of reference here to children whose deceased father has left a will containing provisions for their upbringing and inheritance. The analogy in 3:23–25 primarily has the Jewish nation under the Torah in view. Now Paul has all nations, Jewish and Gentile, in view. Hence the singular pedagogue has become the many "guardians and managers" (ESV). Until the child reaches the age specified in the father's will, others have authority over his or her person and property. The children (and teenagers) must go as the guardians and managers direct and live within the limits they set. This, says Paul, is what life under "the elementary principles of the world" is like. It is a slavish existence but, once again, it is a *temporary* one. A father sets a time in his will at which the minor children will gain authority over their own persons and possessions. In the same way, the Father God had set a time for this transition.

Once again the coming of Christ marks the decisive change. The coming of Christ "under the law" purposefully closed off the parentheses on the Law's role and authority. It cleared the way for the fulfillment of the larger plan of God, the adoption of Jew and Gentile together into God's family. Paul shifts his frame of reference again. The coming of Christ and the sending of the Spirit redeem slaves and make them children in the household of God. Paul is no longer working with an *analogy*. This is the *reality* of the human situation as he sees it.

What are these "elementary principles of the world"? "The world" here is not God's good creation, but "the present evil age" (1:4). "The world" is that bundle of arrangements and powers to which Paul was glad to be crucified and dead (6:14). The Greek word translated as "elementary principles" could have many different meanings depending on the context. Paul has already given us some important context here by naming three opposing pairs of categories in the previous paragraph. They are the categories that divide up reality and, thereby, both make sense of reality and *impose* their order and values on reality. They create hierarchy and structure in a particular society. They orient individuals to behave within that hierarchy and structure a certain way. They are the rules and values of the society into which we are born and that we internalize as we grow up in society. They are the paths and ruts that society has dug out for us, in which we are supposed to live from birth to death. They make us a slave serving "the present evil age," keeping its values and structures alive for the *next* generation to serve!

Both the Torah and any *other* regulatory principles of the world belong in the Galatians' past life. The adult cannot turn back the clock and become a child under the pedagogue or under guardians and managers again. In the same way, the Galatians must take stock of what it means that "the fullness of time" has come with Christ.

1. What would you name as some of society's elementary principles and lines of division that you have internalized? How do these hold you back in terms of discipleship and mission?
2. How would your life change if you allowed Christ to rebuild it from the ground up based on the elementary principles of his kingdom?

FOUR

Slaves No Longer

Galatians 4:6–11 ESV *And because you are sons, God has sent the Spirit of his Son into our hearts, crying, "Abba! Father!"* [7]*So you are no longer a slave, but a son, and if a son, then an heir through God.*

[8]Formerly, when you did not know God, you were enslaved to those that by nature are not gods. [9]But now that you have come to know God, or rather to be known by God, how can you turn back again to the weak and worthless elementary principles of the world, whose slaves you want to be once more? [10]You observe days and months and seasons and years! [11]I am afraid I may have labored over you in vain.

Key Observation. The Holy Spirit assures us that we are God's children and emboldens us to live into the freedom Christ won for us.

Understanding the Word. We are reminded again of the importance of the Holy Spirit for Paul. The believers' *experience* of the Spirit is *evidence* that God has indeed adopted them as sons and daughters. Paul writes as if his converts will have no question in their minds about having had this experience. Nor was this some isolated experience in their lives. Paul writes about the God who "keeps supplying you with the Spirit and working wonders among you" (3:5, author's translation). He writes here about the Spirit that keeps calling out "Abba! Father!" to God within them. The ongoing quality of this action, a characteristic of the Greek verbs used here, almost never makes it into translation.

Abba is *not* a Greek word, however. It is Aramaic, the everyday language that Jesus spoke in Galilee. *Abba* appears only three times in the New Testament. Jesus addresses God as "Abba, Father" in the garden of Gethsemane (Mark 14:36). Paul twice says that the Holy Spirit leads Christian converts to address God in the same way (see also Romans 8:14). Perhaps Jewish Christian evangelists taught this word to their converts. Perhaps the Holy Spirit directly inspired this utterance. Whatever the explanation, the early Christians identified with Jesus' experience of God as Father in a deeply personal and relational way. This is not surprising, since the Spirit was making them one *in* Jesus and one *with* Jesus, the Son. Paul relies here on his converts having this experience of God's paternal love through the Spirit. He urges them now to value that experience and not to let anyone raise any doubts about that experience.

Prison inmates can have great difficulty living on the outside. Some quickly return to crime so as to return to the routine and culture that have become familiar, even comfortable. It doesn't matter anymore that this means prison. Paul is deeply aware that human beings have difficulty leaving other prisons behind as well. Paul's message, however, is that turning back toward prison or slavery is always a stupid choice.

God took the initiative to draw the Galatians into such a close and personal relationship with him that they could call him "Abba, Father." How could they consider throwing this away for the sake of returning to the life of the slave under the elementary principles? Of course, the Galatians had been led to believe that conforming their lives to the Jewish law would be a step forward, not backward. This is what has led them to begin observing some of the Jewish religious festivals. Observing "days and months and seasons and years" recalls the language of the creation story. There the sun, moon, and stars are given "for signs and for seasons and for days and years" (Gen. 1:14). Jews observed the Sabbath, new moon festivals, seasonal events like Passover, and annual events like the New Year. Paul claims that, in submitting to this ritual calendar, the Galatians were returning to their slavery to sun, moon, and stars.

1. How fully has the Holy Spirit opened you up to the experience of calling upon God as your "Abba, Father"? Do you have the Spirit's testimony that you are God's child?
2. What challenges have you and your Christian community faced regarding remaining in the freedom of following the Spirit's leading?

FIVE

An Appeal from Paul's Heart

Galatians 4:12–20 ESV *Brothers, I entreat you, become as I am, for I also have become as you are. You did me no wrong.*
[13]You know it was because of a bodily ailment that I preached the gospel to you at first,
[14]and though my condition was a trial to you, you did not scorn or despise me, but received me as an angel of God, as Christ Jesus.
[15]What then has become of your blessedness? For I testify to you that, if possible, you would have gouged out your eyes and given them to me.
[16]Have I then become your enemy by telling you the truth?
[17]They make much of you, but for no good purpose. They want to shut you out, that you may make much of them.
[18]It is always good to be made much of for a good purpose, and not only when I am present with you,
[19]my little children, for whom I am again in

the anguish of childbirth until Christ is formed in you! [20]I wish I could be present with you now and change my tone, for I am perplexed about you.

Key Observation. Paul is passionate to see Christ take shape fully in each and among all of his converts.

Understanding the Word. Paul makes a very personal appeal to his converts in Galatia. Paul had "become as [the Galatians] are" insofar as he, though born a Jew, relinquished that identity at least to the extent that it would hinder his moving among and reaching out to the Gentile Galatians. As he will write later, "to those outside the law I became as one outside the law . . . that I might win those outside the law" (1 Cor. 9:21 ESV). This is certainly a more gracious approach than that taken by the men from James in Syrian Antioch. Their position is, "become like us, because we're certainly not going to become like you Gentiles." Paul calls now for a little reciprocity from his converts. They should continue to take Paul as their model, not the rival teachers.

Paul recalls their first encounter quite differently from what we read about Paul's missionary work in Galatia in Acts. Paul hadn't even planned on preaching there, but an ailment prevented him from pressing on to his destination. He shows a truly in-Spirited response, however, turning the setback into an opportunity. The Galatians, moreover, respond to him favorably. They might have scorned him, reasoning that a person whose God left him so sick or weak had nothing to offer them in the way of religion. They might have "spat" (the ESV reads "despise") as a means of warding off whatever bad juju had affected Paul adversely. But God broke through to the Galatians through Paul, and they received him honorably as God's apostle. Paul says that they would have dug out their eyes for him—an expression meaning that they would have done anything for him, not a sign that he was having eye trouble. So Paul is left to ask: "What happened that you no longer consider God's favor to rest upon me?" The ESV renders this: "What then has become of your blessedness?" The Greek word rendered "blessedness" means something more like a "pronouncement that someone is blessed." Paul clearly feels betrayed by people who had become very dear friends.

Friends tell one another the truth. This is precisely what Paul has been doing in this letter. If he has been harsh, it is only because he has had to sound the alarm for his friends who are oblivious to the danger of their situation.

The rival teachers, however, have not been acting as genuine friends. They're courting the Galatians only to convince the Galatians that they're still outside of the people of promise. They want the Galatians to court *them* and become *their* followers.

Paul, however, has been courting the Galatians all along with noble intentions. He wants only to see Christ come fully alive in and among them. We should not miss Paul's passion here. He dearly sought this transformation in himself, to the extent that he counted everything else to be rubbish (see Philippians 3:7–11). It is also what he dearly seeks to see happen in the lives of his converts. He uses the image of a woman in labor to express his investment in them and his anguish at this critical stage in their development. Will Christ indeed take shape and be birthed in them, or will their faith be stillborn?

1. How important to you is the formation of Christ in your life? What do your daily priorities and activities say about its importance to you?
2. To what extent do you seek opportunities to advance God's interests even when things do not go according to plan?

WEEK FIVE

GATHERING DISCUSSION OUTLINE

A. **Open session in prayer.** Ask that God would astonish us anew with fresh insight from God's Word and transform us into the disciples that Jesus desires us to become.

B. **View the video for this week's readings.**

C. What were key insights or takeaways that you gained from your reading during the week and from watching the video commentary? In particular, how did these help you to grow in your faith and understanding of Scripture this week? What parts of the Bible lesson or study raised questions for you?

D. **Discuss selected questions from the daily readings.** Invite class members to share key insights or to raise questions that they found to be the most meaningful.

1. **KEY OBSERVATION:** The law of Moses ensured that the seedbed of Israel would be securely in place when the Seed, Christ, finally came into the world.

   DISCUSSION QUESTION: How does Paul's view of the Law's role in Israel's life and in God's plan orient you to reading and valuing the Old Testament?

2. **KEY OBSERVATION:** How society has taught us to categorize, limit, and relate to one another must have no force among those who are "in Christ."

   DISCUSSION QUESTION: What would need to change in your church for it to reflect fully Paul's vision for oneness in Christ?

3. **KEY OBSERVATION:** Christ sets us free from running in the ruts society has dug out for us to make us live out our lives perpetuating its systems and values.

   DISCUSSION QUESTION: What would you name as some of society's elementary principles and lines of division that you have internalized? How do these hold you back in terms of discipleship and mission?

4. **KEY OBSERVATION:** The Holy Spirit assures us that we are God's children and emboldens us to live into the freedom Christ won for us.

   DISCUSSION QUESTION: How fully has the Holy Spirit opened you up to the experience of calling upon God as your "Abba, Father"? Do you have the Spirit's testimony that you are God's child?

5. **KEY OBSERVATION:** Paul is passionate to see Christ take shape fully in each and among all of his converts.

   DISCUSSION QUESTION: How important to you is the formation of Christ in your life? What do your daily priorities and activities say about its importance to you?

E. **As the study concludes, consider specific ways that this week's Bible lessons invite you to grow and call you to change.** How do they call us to think differently? How do they challenge us to change in order to align ourselves with God's work in the world? What specific actions should we take to apply the insights of the lesson into our daily lives? What kind of person does our Bible lesson call us to become?

F. **Close session with prayer.** Emphasize God's ongoing work of transformation in our lives in preparation for loving mission and service in the world. Pray for missing class members as well as for persons whom we need to invite to join our study.

WEEK SIX

Galatians 4:21–5:12

Protect Your Freedom!

ONE

Listening to the Law

Galatians 4:21–24 NIV *Tell me, you who want to be under the law, are you not aware of what the law says? [22]For it is written that Abraham had two sons, one by the slave woman and the other by the free woman. [23]His son by the slave woman was born according to the flesh, but his son by the free woman was born as the result of a divine promise.*

[24]These things are being taken figuratively: The women represent two covenants. One covenant is from Mount Sinai and bears children who are to be slaves: This is Hagar.

Key Observation. The Old Testament no longer has force as Law, but it retains its force as authoritative instruction.

Understanding the Word. Paul does not suggest that anyone throw out the Law. While the Law, or the Old Testament, may not be *normative*, it is still *informative*. It is still the authoritative witness to God's character and purposes. It still reveals a great deal about what righteousness looks like, even if it does not have legal and binding authority. Paul does not want the Galatians to get circumcised or start conforming themselves to the Jewish way of life that the Law prescribes. But he does want the Galatians to *listen* to what the Law, as Scripture, has to say. If they listen carefully to its message, they will know that it is not a mark in the flesh but the power of the Spirit that makes a person Abraham's heir.

Paul refers in broad strokes to the story of Abraham's quest for an heir. He assumes that his readers will be familiar with this story. If you are not, take a moment to read Genesis 15:1–6; 16:1–16; and 21:1–14. Indeed, the rival teachers might have used the story to show that only those who were descended through *Isaac* were Abraham's heirs. This group would include Jews, who claimed to be physically descended from Isaac. It would also include those Gentiles who became Jews through circumcision and Torah observance.

Paul says that this reading is all wrong. If one takes the story only at face value, one will miss its meaning. The story teaches that Abraham's true children and heirs are born in line with God's promise. Those who rely on what human beings can manage for themselves are like Ishmael. Abraham and the slave girl Hagar were able to bring Ishmael into being on their own strength. They relied on the flesh to get this child, and this child proved not to be the heir of the promises. The birth of Isaac was different. Abraham and Sarah couldn't conceive him on their own, but God's power at work in them brought Isaac into existence. To be born in line with Ishmael is to be born into a slavish existence, even as Ishmael was the son of Sarah's slave girl. To be born in line with Isaac is to be born into freedom and to remain in Abraham's true household. Paul presented life under the Law as slavery and the coming of Christ as the introduction of freedom a few paragraphs earlier. That will help support his redrawing of the lines here.

Hagar and Sarah represent two covenants. The rival teachers are promoting the covenant literally carved into the flesh. They are urging the Galatians to make themselves children of Abraham on the basis of what they can accomplish on their own power. They can have themselves circumcised. They can follow some dietary rules. They can keep a calendar of feasts and festivals. But, Paul asserts, God has decreed that the promise would be granted to those who become Abraham's children by trusting God and relying on God's power. This power is none other than the Holy Spirit, the blessing promised through Abraham (see 3:13–14). The genuine sons and daughters of Abraham are those to whom the Spirit has been given (4:6–7).

1. What role does the Old Testament play in your devotional life? To what extent does it speak to you of God's character and purposes?

2. In what ways have you limited your progress in discipleship or activity in mission to what you knew you could do on your own strength?

TWO

Multiplying Abraham's Descendants

Galatians 4:25–31 NIV *Now Hagar stands for Mount Sinai in Arabia and corresponds to the present city of Jerusalem, because she is in slavery with her children.* [26]*But the Jerusalem that is above is free, and she is our mother.* [27]*For it is written: "Be glad, barren woman, you who never bore a child; shout for joy and cry aloud, you who were never in labor; because more are the children of the desolate woman than of her who has a husband."*

[28]*Now you, brothers and sisters, like Isaac, are children of promise.* [29]*At that time the son born according to the flesh persecuted the son born by the power of the Spirit. It is the same now.* [30]*But what does Scripture say? "Get rid of the slave woman and her son, for the slave woman's son will never share in the inheritance with the free woman's son."* [31]*Therefore, brothers and sisters, we are not children of the slave woman, but of the free woman.*

Key Observation. God fulfills his promise to give Abraham countless descendants through Jesus and the church's mission.

Understanding the Word. Paul takes a further step in his interpretation of the stories of Hagar and Sarah. They are no longer two *mothers* but represent mother *cities*. Jews indeed thought of Jerusalem in Judea as their mother city. Paul looks at Jerusalem and all her children and sees people still laboring under slavery to the pedagogue, the Law. He sees people who refuse to step out into the freedom Christ had secured. He claims, however, that all those who are in Christ have a better mother city. This is "the Jerusalem that is above." The description is significant. From a human perspective, this city might be considered the Jerusalem that is yet to come. From God's perspective, however, it already exists in God's realm above. It is a superior mother city since it does not belong to this world, this creation, this present evil age. Paul affirms here what he will say elsewhere: "our citizenship is in heaven" (Phil. 3:20).

Paul recites Isaiah 54:1 as evidence for his claims in verse 26. He may have landed on this passage because the word "barren" suggests a link with Sarah. She is first introduced in Scripture as "barren" (Gen. 11:30). Paul's reading is even more sophisticated, however. The verse he quotes immediately follows the famous Suffering Servant passage in Isaiah 52:13–53:12. There, the Righteous One bears the sins of many, ransoms, and makes them righteous. The Suffering Servant engenders offspring even though he dies. Early Christians, of course, read this passage as a prophecy about Jesus. It was particularly important as a witness to the significance of Jesus' suffering and death. Jesus is the vehicle for fulfilling God's promise of countless descendants to Abraham. Paul's mission to the Gentiles, moreover, is begetting many more children for "the Jerusalem that is above" than the covenant of Moses ever could. And it is doing so in the manner of Isaac's birth—on the basis of trusting God's promise.

Nothing in the Genesis narrative suggests that Ishmael was a danger to Isaac. The Hebrew text of Genesis 21:9 only says that "Sarah saw the son of Hagar the Egyptian . . . laughing" (ESV) or "amusing himself" (author's translation). There is no indication that he was playing with her son, Isaac, certainly not "making fun of . . . Isaac" (NLT). By the time Paul wrote his letter, however, the story had been expanded. Some motive had to be discovered for Sarah's cold-hearted request that Abraham turn Hagar and Ishmael out into the desert! What motive would be better than protecting her own child, Isaac, from Ishmael's violence? Paul can thus speak of Ishmael's persecution of Isaac prefiguring the persecution that Jewish Christians endure from non-Christian Jews. He might also think here of the harassment that he and his converts endure from the rival teachers, who also remain spiritually children of Hagar.

Paul now recites Sarah's request as the command of Scripture. This serves his purposes in two ways. First, the Galatians may hear in this verse a command to break off relations with the rival teachers. Second, Paul subtly warns the Galatians once again of the danger of their position. If they seek to be born into the covenant of Sinai by means of circumcision, they will cut themselves off from the promise and the inheritance!

1. Do your daily interests, activities, and concerns reflect more an identity as a citizen of your earthly country or as a citizen of God's kingdom?
2. Why is it important to Paul to root his claims about Jesus and the significance of his own mission in the Old Testament Scriptures?

THREE
Defacing Grace

Galatians 5:1–4 NIV *It is for freedom that Christ has set us free. Stand firm,*
then, and do not let yourselves be burdened again by a yoke of slavery.
[2]*Mark my words! I, Paul, tell you that if you let yourselves be circumcised,*
Christ will be of no value to you at all. [3]*Again I declare to every man who lets*
himself be circumcised that he is obligated to obey the whole law. [4]*You who are*
trying to be justified by the law have been alienated from Christ; you have fallen
away from grace.

Key Observation. The freedom that cost Jesus so dearly to win for us must be dearly cherished and preserved.

Understanding the Word. Paul arrives at last at his principal proposition. Christ has won for human beings a very costly freedom. Paul has reminded his converts of this throughout his letter. He has pointed again and again to Jesus' giving himself up to death on their behalf (1:4; 2:20; 3:1, 13). It is imperative to value this gift—and honor what it cost Jesus!—by preserving this freedom.

Paul gives equal attention to two dimensions of this freedom. It is both freedom *from* and freedom *for*. It is freedom *from* living as slaves or minor children under the constraints of "the elementary principles of the world" (4:3 ESV). It does not matter whether those constraints were laid out by the Torah or the operating principles and values of Gentile societies. It is freedom *for* a new quality of relationship with God as "Abba, Father." It is freedom *for* a new quality of life and relationships in community produced by the Holy Spirit's leading and power. Turning back to the law of Moses as the way forward from this point means renouncing all that Christ had accomplished. This is the danger most in view here in Galatians. The freed slave who chooses voluntarily to bend again under "a yoke of slavery" has thrown away the price of his or her ransom. But Paul makes us aware of other forms of slavery to which the ransomed must not return. Turning back to live within the lines and ruts of this world's values and practices is another danger. Turning back to live under the power of our own self-centered and self-serving impulses is another. The latter will occupy Paul in 5:13–6:10.

Verses 2 through 4 outline the negative consequences of failing to heed Paul's advice. Paul lays out these consequences primarily in terms of the grace relationship his converts have enjoyed with Christ. Underlying this paragraph is a piece of socially learned logic that Paul and his converts shared. How a person treats a gift and responds to the giver will affect his or her relationship with that giver. Both "grace" and "faith" are words that are native to this kind of relationship in Paul's world. "Faith" speaks about trust in the giver, trust in the value of his or her gifts, trust that he or she will deliver what he or she has promised. Will the Galatians continue to exhibit this faith, this trust, in Jesus?

Here is the root problem with their turning to the law of Moses at this point as the way forward to being accounted righteous by God. It shows a stunning *lack* of trust in Jesus and in the value of the gift of the Spirit. It exhibits distrust that Jesus can, indeed, bring them to the promised goal of righteousness. To exhibit such distrust to so selfless a benefactor is to break off the grace relationship. It is an insult for which there is no remedy. Thus if the Galatians persist down this path, "Christ will be of no benefit to you" (5:2). This includes losing the saving benefits of his death. To be "obliged to obey the entire law" (5:3) includes having to return to depending even on its system of sacrifices. They would be cut off from all that Jesus has done or would do for them.

1. In what ways have you taken care to preserve, and in what ways have you been compromising, your freedom in Christ?
2. How would your priorities and practices change if you began to trust Jesus and the Spirit, and thus follow their lead, entirely?

FOUR

Faith That Works

Galatians 5:5–6 NIV *For through the Spirit we eagerly await by faith the righteousness for which we hope. [6]For in Christ Jesus neither circumcision nor uncircumcision has any value. The only thing that counts is faith expressing itself through love.*

Key Observation. The faith that saves is the faith that leads us to invest ourselves in loving action.

Understanding the Word. Paul has not been taking issue with the rival teachers' or the Galatians' *goal.* All parties here are looking for the way to fall in line with God's righteousness. They are looking for the way to become the people that God will acquit at the last judgment. Paul's issue is with the effective means to attain this goal. The Torah-driven life cannot be the means. If that had been the way forward, what was the point of God's Son dying on a cross (2:21)? It is the Spirit-driven life that leads to this good end. Paul offers these two verses as support for his primary proposition in 5:1. The Galatians can "stand firm," since the path that faith in Jesus has opened up will lead to their attaining "the righteousness for which we hope."

Notice that there are two phrases in verse 5 that give details about how we arrive at this righteousness. It comes about not only "by faith" but also "through the Spirit." Trusting Jesus and the work of the Holy Spirit go hand-in-hand in Paul's understanding of the Christian life. Specifically, trusting Jesus gives us access to the priceless gift that Jesus offers. This gift is the Holy Spirit to live with us and in us (3:13–14; 4:6–7). The Holy Spirit allows us, like Paul, to come alive to God in a way that the law of Moses could not bring about (2:19). The Holy Spirit is at work making Christ come alive within us "until Christ is formed in [us]" (4:19) and God can recognize his Righteous One in each of us. Paul's gospel is not about getting off the hook with God at the judgment. It is about getting right with God and in line with God over the course of our lives so that we have nothing to fear at the judgment. It is about how God transforms us so that we will be at home in God's kingdom, "where righteousness is at home" (2 Peter 3:13).

This has nothing to do, however, with getting in line with the rules and regulations that marked Israel off as Israel. Whether a person is a Jew or a Gentile makes no difference, and the Torah is all about living as a Jew. Paul reduces the significance of these ethnic lines to the absurd. The condition of a foreskin doesn't convey any power for righteousness. What makes all the difference is that level of trust in Jesus that translates into loving action.

Too many Christians think that Paul sets faith over good works. The latter are regarded, then, as bad or, at best, optional. True, Paul set faith *in Christ* over against works *of the law* for all the reasons we have already explored. But faith in Christ also works! Paul does not say that what counts is faith. What counts is "faith *working* though love" (5:6), faith investing itself in loving action. This is the formula for righteousness and, therefore, justification in Paul's gospel. As it is attained only by the Spirit's guidance and empowerment, it ever remains the result of grace—of Christ's gift.

1. What roles do grace, faith, Jesus, the Spirit, and transformation play in Paul's gospel of how God intervened to set all things right?
2. In what ways has your trust in Jesus manifested in loving action? What would need to change to manifest this more fully?

FIVE

Cutting off the Competition

Galatians 5:7–12 NIV *You were running a good race. Who cut in on you to*
keep you from obeying the truth? [8]That kind of persuasion does not come from
the one who calls you. [9]"A little yeast works through the whole batch of dough."
[10]I am confident in the Lord that you will take no other view. The one who is
throwing you into confusion, whoever that may be, will have to pay the penalty.
[11]Brothers and sisters, if I am still preaching circumcision, why am I still being
persecuted? In that case the offense of the cross has been abolished. [12]As for those
agitators, I wish they would go the whole way and emasculate themselves!

Key Observation. We must remain alert both to ways in which false gospels have thrown us off track and to ways in which the genuine gospel has not shaken us up.

Understanding the Word. In this paragraph, Paul advances his goal for the Galatians in another mode. He is seeking to drive a wedge further between them and the rival teachers. Creating distance between one's audience and the position of opposing speakers often involves creating distance between one's audience and those speakers themselves. This is part and parcel of persuasion—and not just in the ancient world.

Paul uses several images here to capture the impact of the rival teachers on his congregations. The first is running, presumably a race (that is not explicit in the Greek, but reasonable). The rival teachers have cut in on the Galatian Christians' lane. This has made them miss a step and trip up in their obedient response to the gospel. The second is preparing bread. In the ancient world, leaven was more like our sourdough starter than the nice, dry yeast that comes in packages. It smelled bad and, when a little was worked into the lump of dough, transferred its sour properties to the whole. The Galatians are put on notice. If they let in any part of the rival teachers' influence, it will sour the whole enterprise. Paul asserts that their position does not come from God. This is something Paul has spent the last two chapters or more demonstrating. He expresses confidence in his converts as a way of assuring them of his own goodwill. In the same breath he paints the rival teachers once again as agitators or troublemakers. They are people disturbing the health and harmony of the congregations and God will hold them accountable! Paul's closing swipe is admittedly nasty. It is striking that he, though a Jew himself, can place circumcision and castration on the same spectrum. They are both merely mutilations now, different only in degree!

In this paragraph we find another sign that the rival teachers had been employing the same strategy. Verse 11 would make no sense to the hearers unless someone else had already said, "Paul still promotes circumcision. I can't imagine his motives for not telling *you all* about its importance." Paul can readily disprove this slur. The fact that Jewish populations continue to respond to him with hostility demonstrates that he is consistent in his message. Paul may indeed have promoted circumcision and Torah observance in his life prior to encountering the glorified Christ. Since then, however, he has faithfully preserved "the offense of the cross" wherever he has gone. The word rendered "offense" is more colorful in the Greek—"a stumbling block." This offense was not merely the proclamation of a crucified Messiah, though that was hard to swallow. The offense lay also in the implications of the crucified Messiah for the lines between Jew and Gentile and for the line-maker, the Torah. Paul had to trip over the stumbling block of the cross if he was to get up and start out on the right path himself. He won't rob the gospel of that power now, even if it means enduring being flogged in synagogues and being driven out of cities (see 2 Corinthians 11:24; Acts 13:50; 14:2, 19–20).

1. To what extent have you allowed false or partial gospels to infiltrate your theology and your practice? What might you need to get back on track?
2. To what extent has the "offense of the cross" shaken you out of respecting socially learned lines of race, nationalism, gender, and socioeconomic class?

WEEK SIX

GATHERING DISCUSSION OUTLINE

A. **Open session in prayer.** Ask that God would astonish us anew with fresh insight from God's Word and transform us into the disciples that Jesus desires us to become.

B. **View the video for this week's readings.**

C. What were key insights or takeaways that you gained from your reading during the week and from watching the video commentary? In particular, how did these help you to grow in your faith and understanding of Scripture this week? What parts of the Bible lesson or study raised questions for you?

D. **Discuss selected questions from the daily readings.** Invite class members to share key insights or to raise questions that they found to be the most meaningful.

1. **KEY OBSERVATION:** The Old Testament no longer has force as Law, but it retains its force as authoritative instruction.

   DISCUSSION QUESTION: What role does the Old Testament play in your devotional life? To what extent does it speak to you of God's character and purposes?

2. **KEY OBSERVATION:** God fulfills his promise to give Abraham countless descendants through Jesus and the church's mission.

   DISCUSSION QUESTION: Do your daily interests, activities, and concerns reflect more an identity as a citizen of your earthly country or as a citizen of God's kingdom?

3. **KEY OBSERVATION:** The freedom that cost Jesus so dearly to win for us must be dearly cherished and preserved.

   DISCUSSION QUESTION: In what ways have you taken care to preserve, and in what ways have you been compromising, your freedom in Christ?

4. **KEY OBSERVATION:** The faith that saves is the faith that leads us to invest ourselves in loving action.

   DISCUSSION QUESTION: In what ways has your trust in Jesus manifested in loving action? What would need to change to manifest this more fully?

5. **KEY OBSERVATION:** We must remain alert both to ways in which false gospels have thrown us off track and to ways in which the genuine gospel has not shaken us up.

   DISCUSSION QUESTION: To what extent has the "offense of the cross" shaken you out of respecting socially learned lines of race, nationalism, gender, and socioeconomic class?

E. **As the study concludes, consider specific ways that this week's Bible lessons invite you to grow and call you to change.** How do they call us to think differently? How do they challenge us to change in order to align ourselves with God's work in the world? What specific actions should we take to apply the insights of the lesson into our daily lives? What kind of person does our Bible lesson call us to become?

F. **Close session with prayer.** Emphasize God's ongoing work of transformation in our lives in preparation for loving mission and service in the world. Pray for missing class members as well as for persons whom we need to invite to join our study.

WEEK SEVEN

Galatians 5:13–26

The Spirit-Driven Life

ONE

The Freedom to Serve

Galatians 5:13–15 *For you were called to freedom, brothers and sisters; only do not use your freedom as an opportunity for self-indulgence, but through love become slaves to one another. [14]For the whole law is summed up in a single commandment, "You shall love your neighbor as yourself." [15]If, however, you bite and devour one another, take care that you are not consumed by one another.*

Key Observation. The freedom Christ gives is freedom to serve others through loving action, thus fulfilling the Law's highest ideal.

Understanding the Word. In this week's readings, Paul demonstrates why the Galatian Christians do not need to observe the Jewish law to experience freedom from the power of sin. Paul is not addressing people who *want* to sin. Their desire for righteous living is a major motivation to adopt a Law-observant lifestyle. They want to live beyond the pull of their self-centered passions. They want to embody the virtues they know God seeks for in his people. Paul shows them that God's Holy Spirit is a superior guide. The Spirit empowers what the Torah could only demand.

Christ indeed died to bring us into a life of freedom. But freedom is not *license.* Christ did not die to set us loose to live *for* our self-indulgent, self-promoting, self-serving, self-centered impulses and desires. He died to set us free also from living as slaves to those masters. The NRSV uses the term "self-indulgence" here in verse 13 where the NIV and ESV read "flesh." The latter is closer to Paul's word choice, but the NRSV points us in the right direction concerning Paul's meaning. For Paul, the flesh that hangs on our bones is not the problem. *Flesh* is his catchword for that bundle of self-centered drives and cravings that lead us away from righteousness and into sin. We abuse the gift of Christian freedom if we use it to allow the flesh to entrench itself *against* the Spirit in our lives.

After distancing his hearers from the Law as a slavish life, he surprises them by urging them now to express their freedom by serving one another as slaves through loving action. Though this image is admittedly problematic, it captures something essential. Slaves do not live at their own disposal, and Christian freedom must express itself in *voluntarily* putting ourselves at the other person's disposal. As we put ourselves wholly at the disposal of the Spirit, the Spirit puts us wholly at one another's disposal. This is Christ living through us, the One who came to serve rather than to be served (see Mark 10:45). The One who loved us and gave himself for us (see Galatians 1:4; 2:20) now leads us to love and give ourselves for one another. As we do so, we love in the manner of Christ and fulfill the highest ideal of the Law.

This brings Paul to another surprising statement. After working so hard to convince the Galatians not to take up the *doing* of the Law, he shows them that by the proper use of Christian freedom they will still *fulfill* the Law. Paul probably knew of Jesus' summary of the Law as love for God with all one's being and love for neighbor as for oneself (see Mark 12:28–31). Paul holds up the second of these as the core commandment for which the rest of the Law was commentary. Promoting loving action, which always puts the neighbor first and prioritizes his or her good, is what the Law was after all along.

The alternative is not pretty. Paul paints a colorful portrait of the kind of community marked by a dog-eat-dog approach as each individual seeks to advance his or her own ends at another's expense. Better by far to look out for one another than to have to be on the lookout against each other!

1. Reflect on a recent dog-eat-dog exchange with another believer. How could Paul's instructions here have helped lead to a better outcome?

2. What would need to change in your priorities and practice to put yourself more fully at Christ's disposal to serve others as Christ would wish to do through you?

TWO
The Path to Assured Victory

Galatians 5:16–18 *Live by the Spirit, I say, and do not gratify the desires of the flesh. [17]For what the flesh desires is opposed to the Spirit, and what the Spirit desires is opposed to the flesh; for these are opposed to each other, to prevent you from doing what you want. [18]But if you are led by the Spirit, you are not subject to the law.*

Key Observation. The Holy Spirit assures us of living beyond the power and pull of the flesh as we consistently walk in line with the Spirit.

Understanding the Word. The NRSV makes a rookie mistake in translation at this point. It renders *both* verbs in verse 16 as commands. The first verb is indeed a command. Paul tells his converts, "Keep walking in line with the Spirit" (author's translation). He presents the second verb, however, as the *assured result* of following the first command. "Keep walking in line with the Spirit and there's *no way* that you'll fulfill what the flesh desires" (author's translation; compare the ESV and NIV). Paul knows that Christians may still commit sins. He makes provision for the community to deal with this together in 6:1–2. But he also knows that the Spirit is far stronger than the flesh. The Christian who *consistently* gives himself or herself over to the Spirit's leading and empowering will not give himself or herself over to the flesh's impulses. The challenge is to grow into that person that follows the Spirit *consistently*, until the Spirit's impulses become one's natural impulses.

Paul knows the Spirit as an other who can be known, sensed, experienced. It is critically important for a Christian to grow in his or her ability to discern the Holy Spirit and his leading. This begins with the secure trust (faith) that God supplies his Spirit to us freely and lavishly, that Jesus died to open the way for the Spirit to live with us and in us.

Paul presents verse 17 as a further explanation of verse 16. This must guide our interpretation here. Paul is not describing a state of stalemate between the Spirit and the flesh, such that the individual is like a ship at sea, now driven by the wind in one direction, now tossed by the churning waves in another. God has given us his Holy Spirit as the wind that will drive our ship relentlessly against the churning sea of the passions into the harbor of righteousness. This is, moreover, the *Spirit's* war. The Spirit is not a resource given to help us in *our* struggle against the flesh. We have been drafted to fight in the *Spirit's* battle, falling in line with the Spirit as soldiers behind their victorious general.

Verse 18 needs to be heard in the context of Paul's statement about freedom. God is not in the business of freeing people *for* indulging the drives and desires that further deface the image of God in them. God *will* place some restraining force upon the flesh. If we receive and walk in line with the greater force, the Spirit, we will not be placed under the yoke of the inferior force, the Law. The Spirit that leads us to give no place to anger or lust relieves us of the need to hear the commands "You shall not murder" or "You shall not commit adultery" (see Exodus 20:1–17).

The power of the flesh is one factor that makes the removal of the Law's bridle so scary. What will help us restrain this force, if not carefully laid out rules and regulations? This wholesome fear of the flesh gaining the upper hand and making a shipwreck of our faith is probably what drives many Christian groups to formulate new bodies of law for themselves as guardrails for their lives. No drinking, no dancing, no card playing, no movies, no cussing. But if the law of Moses that God instituted was insufficient to tame the power of the flesh, how much less sufficient will any of our rules and regulations prove?

1. When have you recognized the Spirit's leading and experienced the Spirit's empowering when faced with the flesh's promptings?
2. What are your expectations for your own transformation into Christ-likeness in this life? Are these expectations consistent with Paul's in this letter?

THREE
Clear Warning Signs

Galatians 5:19–21 *Now the works of the flesh are obvious: fornication, impurity, licentiousness, [20]idolatry, sorcery, enmities, strife, jealousy, anger, quarrels, dissensions, factions, [21]envy, drunkenness, carousing, and things like these. I am warning you, as I warned you before: those who do such things will not inherit the kingdom of God.*

Key Observation. A transformed life is not optional, but essential. Continuing to allow the flesh to drive us puts eternity in jeopardy.

Understanding the Word. Paul provides a list of the kinds of attitudes and behavior that emerge when the flesh is driving. Each of these "works of the flesh" displays an absence or a perversion of love. Sexual indulgence pursued for its own sake objectifies and uses the other. The vices born of competition and division seek to tear down the other rather than secure the other's interests. Drunken parties anesthetize people to the needs of others. Paul does not pretend to give a comprehensive list. All "things like these" should trigger the alarm that the wrong power is driving the individual and the community. (There are thus *many* self-centered indulgences beyond drinking parties that also stupefy us to the ways in which we could be positively serving others and advancing God's good purposes for them.)

These "works of the flesh" do not manifest themselves merely in the lives of individuals. They are also eruptions in the life of the Christian community. Indeed, it is impossible for the flesh to manifest a good number of these works only in a single individual. It takes at least two people for most of them, and larger numbers for several (like factions). Indeed, if Paul's list has an emphasis, it is on the ways in which the flesh disrupts the harmony of community. This is reinforced by Paul's descriptions of anti-community in this section (5:15, 26). A community of faith decides in interaction after interaction what *kind* of community it will be. Do its members give room for the impulses born of the flesh? The community will be marked (and marred) by divisions, enmity, and other forms of internal competition to get one's own way. Do its members consistently seek to walk in step with the Spirit together? It is far less likely that the community will be marked by people moving in contrary directions and finding themselves at odds with one another.

Paul's list is not best approached as a "things not to do" list (though these are, indeed, things not to do). It is more of a diagnostic tool. When we see quarrels, factions, and combat, we should suspect that the flesh is operative somewhere. It's also not likely to be operative only in *one* party in the conflict. Works of the flesh are provoked by works of the flesh. We incite this beast in one another, but the Spirit can master this beast in all of us together. The Spirit is operative where we seek to secure one another's interests, serve one another in love, and bear ourselves gently and patiently toward one another. What do we do, then, when we see the works of the flesh emerging in our own responses or in those of our sisters and brothers? We need to pause, pray together, and figure out how to let the Spirit take charge in us and among us, all of us, each of us, again.

The consequences of continuing to make room for the works of the flesh are direr than the consequences of turning back to the Law. Those who persist in practicing such things will not inherit God's kingdom! Paul is talking about habitual action rather than single slips. Nevertheless, a transformed life is not optional. It is essential. Being welcomed into God's kingdom at the consummation requires submitting to God's rule through the Spirit now.

1. Reflect on your recent actions, pursuits, and responses in light of Paul's diagnostic list. What changes is the Spirit leading you to make?
2. To what extent do the works of the flesh show up in the life of your faith community? How can you help your sisters and brothers be alert to and deal with these when they arise?

FOUR

Good Signs

Galatians 5:22–24 *By contrast, the fruit of the Spirit is love, joy, peace, patience, kindness, generosity, faithfulness,* [23]*gentleness, and self-control. There is no law against such things.* [24]*And those who belong to Christ Jesus have crucified the flesh with its passions and desires.*

Key Observation. Where all follow the Spirit together, the Spirit creates a community characterized by its winsome fruit.

Understanding the Word. Paul categorizes the second list as "the fruit of the Spirit." Paul's list is again representative, not complete. His language here is important. This is the fruit that the *Spirit* produces when the Spirit is the driving force. It is useful to look at this list as a set of relational values to which we should commit ourselves. It is more in keeping with Paul's own imagery, however, to look at this list as a diagnostic. When the Spirit is driving our common processes and our common life, we see love, joy, peace, patience, and the rest. When we *don't* see love, joy, peace, patience, and the rest manifesting in our common processes and our common life, we need to look closely into what is driving us.

Paul does not pause to define any of these qualities of the Spirit's fruit. He is creating a collective impression of the Spirit-driven community. These are all social virtues. They exist not merely in the individual but between people in interactions and relationships. The impression created by Paul's list of what the Spirit produces is entirely different from that created by his previous list. The kinds of attitudes and behaviors that the flesh churns up and the kind of atmosphere that the Spirit creates are entirely incompatible. The contrasting pictures reinforce Paul's statement about the opposing desires of the two forces. The results of each simply cannot coexist in the same person or in the same space. No law would condemn people whose actions and interactions consistently manifest the fruit that the Spirit produces. Least of all would the law of Moses, which sought to nurture love for neighbor above all else.

A word needs to be said about peace, only because many of us tend to be conflict-avoidant. The Spirit does not produce the fruit of peace among our faith communities as we *avoid* addressing difficult topics or avoid having the difficult conversations. Rather, the Spirit produces peace *in the midst of* addressing difficult issues. We look to the Spirit to supply us with the patience, the gentleness, and the generosity that we all need to address these issues together in love.

Christ's death on our behalf becomes a death in which we can—and must—participate. Those who have been plunged into Christ have also died with Christ. Specifically, they have died to the kind of life that the flesh seeks to nurture. They have died with Christ to self-serving, self-gratifying, self-promoting agendas. They live a new life now in the Spirit. Pastors in some theological traditions tend to perpetually reinforce the Christian's identity as a sinner. Paul, however, reinforces Christian identity as that of a person who is "dead to sin" (Rom. 6:11). Here Paul speaks of this identity as someone who has died, in union with Christ, to the flesh along with its passions and yearnings. I *was* a sinner, but sin is no longer my native inclination. I may indeed still sin. But this has become *unnatural* to me, as unnatural as a kick from a corpse. The Christian is someone in whom Christ is coming to life or taking shape more and more fully. Our transformation is in the hands of the Spirit, for whom the flesh is no match.

1. When have you experienced the Spirit producing its fruit in your own life and in your interactions with other believers?
2. What disciplines and practices can help position you to attend to the Spirit's leading more consistently, so that its fruit will be more evident in your interactions?

FIVE

Keeping in Step with the Spirit

Galatians 5:25–26 *If we live by the Spirit, let us also be guided by the Spirit.* [26]*Let us not become conceited, competing against one another, envying one another.*

Key Observation. Paul calls us to allow the Spirit to reorder our values, practices, and ways of relating from the ground up.

Understanding the Word. The death and resurrection of the Messiah loom large in Paul's thinking for many reasons. One of these is the gift that God gives to those who join themselves to Christ to participate in that death and resurrection. The believer dies with Christ to flesh-driven impulses and desires. The believer rises to a new life in the Spirit. He or she comes alive to God in a decisively new way. He or she comes alive to the overwhelming love of Jesus, who gave himself for us. This is the new reality that shapes our new lives. This is the act of grace that calls forth from us a response of gratitude, to live no longer for ourselves but for him who died and was raised on our behalf (see 2 Corinthians 5:15).

Since we are dead to what formerly drove us and alive now by the Spirit's working, the Spirit must become the driving force for this new life. Most translations, including the NRSV, hide a meaningful word-play in the Greek. The verb translated "let us also be guided" in 5:25 is related to the noun translated as "elementary principles" in 4:3 (ESV). The society in which we grew up laid out before us its fundamental ordering principles and practices. We witnessed (and still witness) these principles and practices being lived out around us, to an unfortunate extent *among* us. Christ died to free us from slavery to those ordering principles. These include the ordering principles of ethnic divisions, caste and class divisions, and the differing evaluations of male and female. They include notions of where family ends, how money is to be saved and spent, where religion belongs and doesn't belong. The Spirit is given to us to lead us into God's new ordering of human community. The Spirit must become the fundamental ordering principle for the Christ-follower. As we walk in line with the Spirit, the Spirit constructs new ways of being human together, new values to pursue for human community. The Spirit cuts new pathways for us that lead us out from the ruts that had been carved for us—and *in* us—by the world. He brings our individual lives and our life in community in line with God's righteousness.

What is required of us, if we are to allow the Spirit to order our steps? We need to exercise vigilance over our own impulses. When we recognize the impulses of the flesh, we need to turn immediately to the Spirit for timely help and power to squelch those impulses and fall in step instead with the Spirit's better direction. We need to be committed to diligent and disciplined *dying*. We need to identify and die to those self-centered drives that keep churning up the mucky works of the flesh. We need to reorient ourselves regularly so that we are consciously and consistently seeking the Spirit's leading together, submitting all that we are and all that concerns us to the Spirit.

Once again Paul glances at the alternative; once again it is not pretty. Paul's world was an antagonistic one. The verb rendered "competing" here might better have been rendered "challenging," seeking to gain honor at another's expense. The flip side of this is "envying," harboring the bitter desire to see others *not* prosper. Being filled with the Spirit, however, is the antidote to being too full of ourselves—and to the toxins this produces in our communities.

1. What differences can you identify between the expectations and practices society has laid out for your life and those the Spirit would lay out?

2. To what extent, and in what ways, are you walking more in line with the world's well-worn patterns than the Spirit's groundbreaking paths?

WEEK SEVEN

GATHERING DISCUSSION OUTLINE

A. **Open session in prayer.** Ask that God would astonish us anew with fresh insight from God's Word and transform us into the disciples that Jesus desires us to become.

B. **View the video for this week's readings.**

C. What were key insights or takeaways that you gained from your reading during the week and from watching the video commentary? In particular, how did these help you to grow in your faith and understanding of Scripture this week? What parts of the Bible lesson or study raised questions for you?

D. **Discuss selected questions from the daily readings.** Invite class members to share key insights or to raise questions that they found to be the most meaningful.

1. **KEY OBSERVATION:** The freedom Christ gives is freedom to serve others through loving action, thus fulfilling the Law's highest ideal.

   DISCUSSION QUESTION: What would need to change in your priorities and practice to put yourself more fully at Christ's disposal to serve others as Christ would wish to do through you?

2. **KEY OBSERVATION:** The Holy Spirit assures us of living beyond the power and pull of the flesh as we consistently walk in line with the Spirit.

   DISCUSSION QUESTION: When have you recognized the Spirit's leading and experienced the Spirit's empowering when faced with the flesh's promptings?

3. **KEY OBSERVATION:** A transformed life is not optional, but essential. Continuing to allow the flesh to drive us puts eternity in jeopardy.

   DISCUSSION QUESTION: Reflect on your recent actions, pursuits, and responses in light of Paul's diagnostic list. What changes is the Spirit leading you to make?

4. **KEY OBSERVATION:** Where all follow the Spirit together, the Spirit creates a community characterized by its winsome fruit.

   DISCUSSION QUESTION: What disciplines and practices can help position you to attend to the Spirit's leading more consistently, so that its fruit will be more evident in your interactions?

5. **KEY OBSERVATION:** Paul calls us to allow the Spirit to reorder our values, practices, and ways of relating from the ground up.

   DISCUSSION QUESTION: What differences can you identify between the expectations and practices society has laid out for your life and those the Spirit would lay out?

E. **As the study concludes, consider specific ways that this week's Bible lessons invite you to grow and call you to change.** How do they call us to think differently? How do they challenge us to change in order to align ourselves with God's work in the world? What specific actions should we take to apply the insights of the lesson into our daily lives? What kind of person does our Bible lesson call us to become?

F. **Close session with prayer.** Emphasize God's ongoing work of transformation in our lives in preparation for loving mission and service in the world. Pray for missing class members as well as for persons whom we need to invite to join our study.

WEEK EIGHT

Galatians 6:1–18

Closing Advice, Attacks, and Affirmations

ONE

The Law of the Messiah

Galatians 6:1–2 ESV *Brothers, if anyone is caught in any transgression, you who are spiritual should restore him in a spirit of gentleness. Keep watch on yourself, lest you too be tempted. 2Bear one another's burdens, and so fulfill the law of Christ.*

Key Observation. We depend on one another to help us remain in tune with the Spirit and aware of the flesh's deceitfulness.

Understanding the Word. Paul now gives some specific instructions concerning how to keep walking in the Spirit together. Paul expects Christians who follow the Spirit to live a life of victory over the pull and power of the flesh. He expects the Spirit's fruit to be the new normal for Christian life and Christian community. However, he also knows that individual believers will not be *entirely* consistent in following the Spirit in *every* situation.

One of the safeguards that God has put in place for each believer, who might prove susceptible to the flesh at one point or another, is the intervention of the community of faith. We depend upon our sisters and brothers in Christian community to help us stay in step with the Spirit. We need them to help us get back on track when we take a misstep. Conversely, our sister or brother in Christ depends on *our* willingness to do the same for him or her. Several currents in Western society run counter to the New Testament vision for community. One of these is the invisible barrier that surrounds matters that are considered private and none of someone else's business. This is, however, one of the *world's* organizing principles, not the Spirit's. Many churchgoers are reluctant to cross that barrier. They are not reluctant, however, to talk among themselves about the sin someone else in the community has committed. This practice harms both the individual who has sinned and the community of faith.

Paul's solution is more direct. Those who *are* in touch with the Spirit's leading should approach the believer who has fallen *out* of touch with the Spirit's leading. They should help him or her discover how the flesh has made him or her miss a step. They should do this gently, manifesting one variety of the Spirit's fruit. They should help the individual reawaken to the Spirit's leading and get back on track. Paul instructs us to keep watch over our own souls in the process. He reminds us we are equally susceptible to sin. This keeps our hearts humble and gentle toward our erring sister or brother. There is no room for harshness or feeling superior when intervening in the life of a fellow believer. There is room only for renewed vigilance on our own part against the inroads the flesh seeks to make.

Such watchful care and investment in one another is one example of how we may keep bearing one another's burdens. Paul would no doubt extend this to *all* experiences of life that weigh down our sister or brother. Carrying someone else's luggage was the work of a slave, when one was available. Doing so voluntarily is the work of love. Paul is pointing here to the ways in which we are to "serve one another as slaves through love" (5:13, author's translation). The "law of Christ" may point to Jesus' elevation of the command to love one's neighbor as oneself (5:14). Lifting another's burden is a practical manifestation of this love, taking on the neighbor's burden as one's own. It may also point to Jesus' *example* as our new law or norm. His self-giving, other-centered love takes shape in us as we bear one another's burdens.

1. When has another Christian intervened healthfully to draw you back from some sinful practice or situation?

2. Who in your faith community might benefit from your reaching out to help carry some burden of some kind?

TWO

Know Thyself

Galatians 6:3–6 ESV *For if anyone thinks he is something, when he is nothing, he deceives himself. [4]But let each one test his own work, and then his reason to boast will be in himself alone and not in his neighbor. [5]For each will have to bear his own load.*

[6]Let the one who is taught the word share all good things with the one who teaches.

Key Observation. Our life of serving as Christ served, not our inflated opinions about ourselves, will bring honor for eternity.

Understanding the Word. Paul continues his instructions with a saying that many in his audience might have recognized. Philosophers spoke about our tendency to form too high an opinion of ourselves. Plato wrote against the folly of people who think themselves to be something when they're nothing. Paul introduces this saying as an argument in favor of bearing one another's burdens. If we think ourselves too important to get involved with carrying another believer's burdens, we're deceiving ourselves. We don't yet know the Lord we follow. He's not yet really taking shape within us.

The next verse is a bit difficult to unpack. First, we generally view boasting as a negative practice. Paul, however, seems to think that *some* boasting is alright. Honor is an important value in Paul's culture, and people lay claim to honor. Paul wants to make sure here that Christians lay claim to honor rightly. It is based, first, on "[our] own work." It is *not* based on our imagined superiority to another person, whose burden we are too important to help carry. It is based on what *I* have done that shows Christ taking shape within me. It is *not* based on something I get someone else to do. Paul may already be thinking about the rival teachers. He will shortly accuse them of trying to make trophies out of the Galatians by getting them to accept circumcision (6:13). It is likely that Paul does not think of this claim to honor as something we would make every day. Rather, it is likely that he is thinking about our having a claim to honor on the Last Day (see 2 Corinthians 1:14; Philippians 2:16; 1 Thessalonians 2:19). Elsewhere in Paul's writings, it is only on *that* day that the value of every work will be reliably shown. It is also on *that* day that each of us will have to bear his or her own load.

Paul had just urged us to help carry one another's burdens. Now he asserts that we will only be able to bear our *own* load. This is the difference between the now of everyday life and the then of the judgment. We can and must share the weight of life's burdens throughout the course of this life. We will ultimately stand before God as people responsible each for himself or herself, answering for the ways in which we have used or abused life and grace. There will also be no reward for having done better than a fellow believer. In this way, the saying in verse 5 supports the exhortation in verse 4.

Some people in the house churches took on specialized roles rather early. Paul refers to a few Christians who are particularly tasked with teaching the Word to the group. These believers may have had to reduce their activity in the workplace to devote themselves to study and ministry. Paul urges those who are benefitting from them to show ongoing reciprocity. This is also a further example of mutual burden-bearing. Some in the group are bearing a larger part of the burden of grounding and equipping the saints. The rest are tasked with bearing the burden of helping to support these individuals so that their investment in the group can continue.

1. When have you avoided bearing another believer's burden because you thought it was beneath you or because you were too busy with more pressing matters?
2. To what extent are you taking responsibility for your own progress in discipleship? How?

THREE

Sowing for a Good Harvest

Galatians 6:7–10 ESV *Do not be deceived: God is not mocked, for whatever one sows, that will he also reap. [8]For the one who sows to his own flesh will from the flesh reap corruption, but the one who sows to the Spirit will from the Spirit reap eternal life. [9]And let us not grow weary of doing good, for in due season we* *will reap, if we do not give up.* [10]*So then, as we have opportunity, let us do good to everyone, and especially to those who are of the household of faith.*

Key Observation. What we do with our lives and energies on this side of Jesus' dying for us and gifting us with his Spirit has eternal consequences.

Understanding the Word. Some may be wary about the freedom in the Spirit that Paul proclaims. Won't people abuse this freedom to get away with more than they could under the Torah? Has Paul thrown genuine accountability out the window? Paul says that there is no such danger. The integrity of life in the Spirit is guaranteed by the fact that God knows all things. He is the One "unto whom all hearts are open, all desires known, and from whom no secrets are hid."[4] We cannot fool God. We cannot continue to make room for the flesh under the guise of Christian freedom without consequences. If we tell ourselves otherwise, we are simply deceiving ourselves.

Paul brings this truth home with a proverb drawn from agriculture. Crop after crop, year after year, proves the saying true: we reap precisely what we sow. He applies this to the contrast between the crop produced by the flesh and the fruit of the Spirit that had dominated 5:16–26. Paul is once again not talking about isolated acts that are out of character for us. He is talking about life trajectories. If we keep giving ourselves over to do what the flesh would propel us to do, we will harvest all that the flesh can provide. The ESV reads "corruption." The meaning is decay, the rottenness that befalls our physical flesh in the grace. That is finally the only reward that the flesh can offer to its devotees. If we keep giving ourselves over to what the Spirit would impel us to do, we will harvest what God's Holy Spirit can provide. This is life beyond the fate of our mortal flesh—eternal life. Giving oneself over more and more to the others-centered love that Jesus displayed is the way to secure one's life for eternity. In the end, Paul does not disagree with Jesus on the topic of arriving at safety or salvation. He is not, however, teaching people that they earn their own salvation. He is urging us to give ourselves over fully to the Holy Spirit of God and let Jesus take shape in us.

---

4. *The Book of Common Prayer* (New York: Oxford University, 2007), 355.

Paul urges believers to continue doing what is noble as long as we have life and breath to do so. The assurance of the outcome, the harvest of eternal life, should suffice to overcome any weariness in thus investing oneself. He defines two circles of benevolence. The inner circle contains fellow believers—the "household of faith." Many Christ-followers now, even as in the first century, have lost their networks of support because of their faith. Their Christian family *must* take up the slack if they are to persevere. The larger circle takes us into the area of mission, loving those who do not yet love Christ.

Our ideas about salvation must make room for paragraphs from Scripture like this one. Christians are not immune from the consequences of their actions. They are not somehow more at liberty to indulge in unrighteous living than people who do not call God's Son their friend. If we think this way, we are making a mockery of God's provision. The death of Jesus and the gift of the Spirit are intended to lead us into a life of righteousness. Let us indeed invest ourselves in doing good while we have an opportunity!

1. How fully do you invest your time and resources in doing good for your family in Christ? For those beyond?
2. What might you change in your life to sow more fully and more consistently in the Spirit?

FOUR

A Matter of Motives

Galatians 6:11–13 ESV *See with what large letters I am writing to you with my own hand. [12]It is those who want to make a good showing in the flesh who would force you to be circumcised, and only in order that they may not be persecuted for the cross of Christ. [13]For even those who are circumcised do not themselves keep the law, but they desire to have you circumcised that they may boast in your flesh.*

Key Observation. Paul identifies two enemies of faithful witness and obedience. These are the desire to look good by worldly standards and to avoid encountering hostility for Christ's sake.

Understanding the Word. As Paul ends his letter, he attends to three basic tasks. He gives the Galatians a few more reasons to doubt the reliability of the rival teachers. He provides some good evidence that they should cease to doubt his. He repeats some of the key points of the letter's argument.

As Paul transitions from the body of his letter, he calls attention to the size of the letters he has been scribbling. It has not been the neat and economical writing of a professional secretary. Rather, it is the oversized scrawl of a writer who is personally and emotionally invested in the audience and in the outcome. The rival teachers, on the other hand, are not invested in the audience at all. Paul asserts that they are looking out only for their own interests. They have two related goals for winning the Galatian Christians over to a Torah-observant lifestyle. Positively, it will make them look good in the eyes of most Jews, whether Christian or otherwise. Negatively, it will allow them to avoid persecution at the hands of their fellow Jews.

Paul knew firsthand about persecution. He understood the motives of the persecutors, having been one himself. The blessings and curses of Deuteronomy, which proved true again and again in the Jews' history, taught a vital lesson. The fortunes of Israel depend upon Jews observing the law of Moses. Paul understands the distress and pain of *being* persecuted. This was his own lot after his encounter with Christ. On the one hand, Paul does not have access to all the motives of his rivals. They might well believe that they *are* seeking the Galatians' good by bringing them into alignment with the law of Moses. On the other hand, Paul understands the power of the internal pressures that keep good Jews acting like good Jews. He asserts that these pressures can't be ignored when assessing what is driving his rivals. It would take a great deal of courage for them to dare to think differently about the Law themselves. Paul says that they don't have that.

It is not clear what Paul means when he says that the circumcised do not actually keep the Law themselves. Is he referring to the command to love their neighbor as themselves? He regards his rivals to be driving the Galatians toward a slavish existence—hardly a loving act. Is he thinking about their performance of the Torah from his own perspective as a Pharisee? Most Jews fell short of this sect's standards. Is he referring to the sacrifices and purifications that the Law prescribes? The rival teachers would have ceased to observe these, believing Christ's death to have been decisive in that regard. Whichever cause is foremost in his mind, the point is clear. It is not a sincere commitment to the Torah that drives the rivals. It is cowardice and a desire to please their own people.

1. When have you held back from obedience and witness out of concern for what other people might think?
2. How much of your activity is geared toward looking good to worldly eyes, and how much to being honored in God's sight?

FIVE

What Really Matters

Galatians 6:14–18 ESV *But far be it from me to boast except in the cross of our Lord Jesus Christ, by which the world has been crucified to me, and I to the world. [15]For neither circumcision counts for anything, nor uncircumcision, but a new creation. [16]And as for all who walk by this rule, peace and mercy be upon them, and upon the Israel of God.*

[17]From now on let no one cause me trouble, for I bear on my body the marks of Jesus.

[18]The grace of our Lord Jesus Christ be with your spirit, brothers. Amen.

Key Observation. Dying with Christ, we die to the world's power to order our lives. We are free to become fully God's new creation.

Understanding the Word. Paul will not turn other people into his trophies. He makes his boast only in Christ's cross. Paul had renounced the honor that he enjoyed on the basis of his life "in the world" (see 1:13–14). He seeks honor now only in God's estimation. That honor is revealed most clearly in the crucified Messiah. The cross shows how upside down the world's values are. It shows how misplaced its esteem is. It gave the most degrading station to the person most honored in God's sight, as the resurrection would prove. The cross of Christ reveals what God most values. Serving is the path to distinction. Giving oneself away is the path to securing one's self for eternity.

The cross broke the hold that this world and its values held on Paul and his attraction to the world's honor. It set him free at last to find true and lasting honor before God.

Paul once again declares circumcision and uncircumcision equally irrelevant on this side of dying with Christ. Circumcision and uncircumcision are a pair of categories promoted by "the elementary principles of the world" (4:3 ESV). It creates the divisive pair of Jew and Gentile, a division of humanity that no longer has value in Christ (see Galatians 3:26–28). Paul's crucifixion to the world included his death to all the ordering principles of the world. This is a death in which all disciples must share if they are to be free to follow where the Spirit leads. The only thing that has value now is the new creation. This new creation takes shape as Christ takes shape within the believer. He or she takes on the image of the new Adam, Jesus, in whom God's image is perfectly borne. The parallelism between this verse and 5:6 suggests that "new creation" is what comes into being as "faith working through love." Human community is renewed.

The principle Paul lays down in 6:15 becomes a "rule" in the sense of yardstick or measuring rod. He calls his hearers one final time to leave behind the world's ordering principles. He calls them to march straight toward the truth that the gospel proclaims and calls into being. The ESV and NRSV treat those "who walk by this rule" and "the Israel of God" as two separate bodies (5:16). Is Paul pronouncing this closing blessing on one or two groups? The NIV is probably more correct to identify those "who walk by this rule" *as* "the Israel of God." Paul has spent the letter demonstrating that those who are in Christ are the people of promise, the genuine heirs of Abraham. It is highly unlikely that Paul would suddenly make an about-face at the end of his letter to give special mention to ethnic Israel. There is no longer Jew nor Greek.

As proof of his reliability and sincerity, Paul points to the scars on his body. They were inflicted to shame Paul, but he regards them as marks of honor. He has been true to his master, Jesus. He has not altered the gospel to please people and avoid their hostility. We would do well to remember our many sisters and brothers across the globe who bear such marks on their own bodies because of their fidelity toward Christ.

Paul closes his letter with a wish that grace would remain with his sisters and brothers in Galatia. Indeed, grace is at stake in their situation. He dearly hopes that they will continue to show trust in Jesus and sufficiently value his gifts.

1. To what extent are you still coloring within the lines that your society has drawn for you?
2. What marks on your life, if not your body, are evidence of your sincerity and commitment to follow Christ?

WEEK EIGHT

GATHERING DISCUSSION OUTLINE

A. **Open session in prayer.** Ask that God would astonish us anew with fresh insight from God's Word and transform us into the disciples that Jesus desires us to become.

B. **View the video for this week's readings.**

C. What were key insights or takeaways that you gained from your reading during the week and from watching the video commentary? In particular, how did these help you to grow in your faith and understanding of Scripture this week? What parts of the Bible lesson or study raised questions for you?

D. **Discuss selected questions from the daily readings.** Invite class members to share key insights or to raise questions that they found to be the most meaningful.

1. **KEY OBSERVATION:** We depend on one another to help us remain in tune with the Spirit and aware of the flesh's deceitfulness.

   DISCUSSION QUESTION: When has another Christian intervened healthfully to draw you back from some sinful practice or situation?

2. **KEY OBSERVATION:** Our life of serving as Christ served, not our inflated opinions about ourselves, will bring honor for eternity.

   DISCUSSION QUESTION: When have you avoided bearing another believer's burden because you thought it was beneath you or because you were too busy with more pressing matters?

3. **KEY OBSERVATION:** What we do with our lives and energies on this side of Jesus' dying for us and gifting us with his Spirit has eternal consequences.

   DISCUSSION QUESTION: How fully do you invest your time and resources in doing good for your family in Christ? For those beyond?

4. **KEY OBSERVATION:** Paul identifies two enemies of faithful witness and obedience. These are the desire to look good by worldly standards and to avoid encountering hostility for Christ's sake.

   DISCUSSION QUESTION: When have you held back from obedience and witness out of concern for what other people might think?

5. **KEY OBSERVATION:** Dying with Christ, we die to the world's power to order our lives. We are free to become fully God's new creation.

   DISCUSSION QUESTION: To what extent are you still coloring within the lines that your society has drawn for you?

E. **As the study concludes, consider specific ways that this week's Bible lessons invite you to grow and call you to change.** How do they call us to think differently? How do they challenge us to change in order to align ourselves with God's work in the world? What specific actions should we take to apply the insights of the lesson into our daily lives? What kind of person does our Bible lesson call us to become?

F. **Close session with prayer.** Emphasize God's ongoing work of transformation in our lives in preparation for loving mission and service in the world. Pray for missing class members as well as for persons whom we should invite to participate in future studies.

FOR FURTHER READING

deSilva, David A. *Transformation: The Heart of Paul's Gospel.* Bellingham, WA: Lexham Press, 2014.

———. *The Letter to the Galatians.* New International Commentary on the New Testament. Grand Rapids: Eerdmans, 2018.

Gorman, Michael J. *Inhabiting the Cruciform God.* Grand Rapids: Eerdmans, 2009.

Keener, Craig. *Galatians.* New Cambridge Bible Commentary. Cambridge: Cambridge University Press, 2018.

Oakes, Peter. *Galatians.* Paideia Commentaries. Grand Rapids: Baker Academic, 2015.

Reeves, Rodney. *Spirituality According to Paul.* Downers Grove: InterVarsity Press, 2011.

Witherington III, Ben. *Grace in Galatia: A Commentary on Paul's Letter to the Galatians.* Grand Rapids: Eerdmans, 1998.

www.ingramcontent.com/pod-product-compliance
Ingram Content Group UK Ltd.
Pitfield, Milton Keynes, MK11 3LW, UK
UKHW021401070726
13610UKWH00012B/67

9 781628 246919